TRULY A PERSON, TRULY GOD

ADRIAN THATCHER

TRULY A PERSON, TRULY GOD

A Post-Mythical View of Jesus

First published in Great Britain in 1990 by
SPCK
Holy Trinity Church
Marylebone Road
London NW1 4DU

British Library Cataloguing in Publication Data

Thatcher, Adrian
   Truly a person, truly God.
   1. Jesus Christ
   I. Title
   232
   ISBN 0-281-04446-5

Typeset by Inforum Typesetting, Portsmouth
Printed in Great Britain by Biddles Ltd, Guildford and Kings Lynn

CONTENTS

ACKNOWLEDGEMENTS

First and foremost I wish to thank Grace, my wife, and John, my son, for their patience and understanding while I have been writing the present work. Only they know how many hours which could have been spent happily with them were spent instead in my study.

The gestation period of *Truly a Person, Truly God* has been long. The scattered thoughts which it brings together are the product of my teaching during the twelve years I have been part of the Religious Studies and Philosophy department at the College of St Mark and St John, Plymouth. My former colleagues Andrew Bebb and Frank Gillies commented helpfully on an earlier version of the present book. So did John Macquarrie, once my supervisor at Oxford, and David Watson, of Bristol University.

I am grateful to students of Religious Studies and Philosophy at St Mark and St John for all I have learned from them; also to students of the Open University. I have taught philosophy on three successive Arts Foundation courses in the Open University: some of the philosophical material in this book derives from interests which began there. The Research Committee of the College awarded me a term off in 1984 when the foundations for the present study were laid. My present departmental colleagues Paul Grosch, Gaynor Pollard and Elizabeth Stuart have provided much encouragement and a vigorous, harmonious atmosphere where the sharing of theological and philosophical ideas is always placed above the many administrative chores.

I have gained much from some further advice from John Macquarrie, and I have been grateful for the interest and encouragement shown to me by Paul Avis. Grace Jantzen read the whole manuscript in draft. The work has been much improved as a result of her numerous concise and detailed criticisms.

Adrian Thatcher
June 1989

CHAPTER 1

The Method

Christians believe that Jesus Christ is truly God and truly man. How a historical individual can be both a human being and a divine Person has always been a puzzle which calls for godly bewilderment from the believer and intellectual humility from the theologian. This book develops a novel approach to the central assertions of Christian faith about Jesus. It will show that recent explorations of what a human person is are able to advance Christian reflection on what a divine Person is. It will build up a series of analogies between the reality of the human person and the reality of the divine Person, God the Son.

In the last two decades British theology has given most of the intellectual difficulties engendered by the incarnation a good airing. Some theologians have given up belief in the incarnation altogether, while others have assailed it as counter-productive to the commendation of the faith, logically impossible, unintelligible, and so on.[1] But this book is not another response to *The Myth of God Incarnate*, nor a contribution to the 'continuing debate', if the 'debate' is an argument between scholars about whether Jesus is God or whether it is necessary for Christians to assume so. Instead it proposes and develops a way of understanding the basic Christian claims about Jesus, which, if successful, also avoids the twin temptations of modern Christology, viz. reduction of the full divinity of Christ to something more manageable (liberalism), and repetition of the ancient formulae without regard for the vastly different thought-world of today (conservatism). The approach to Christology which is developed in these pages assumes that the Church has something momentous to commend (that Jesus Christ is truly God and truly man), and that what is commended can be understood (and not just by a small band of scholars writing for each other).

The stance which will be developed is that the belief that Jesus Christ is fully a human being and fully God is essential to the faith, intelligible to Christians and non-Christians, and true. It owes an equal debt to theological liberalism and conservatism and tries to integrate the best elements of each. An approach to understanding the deity and humanity of Christ and their relationship is needed which goes beyond the polarization in Christology between the dilution of the liberals and the defensiveness of the conservatives,

and this book is an attempt to provide it. The liberals, ever anxious
to make connections between the tradition about Jesus and modern secularized consciousness, are in danger of giving up the very
truth they want to share; the conservatives, anxious to defend the
tradition about Jesus from dilution, are in danger of sharing that
truth with no one but themselves. A Christology which serves the
Church and helps it to shine the light of Christ upon the world is
likely to be one which takes tradition and communication with
equal seriousness, and lets itself be shaped by the different demands of each. All worthwhile doctrinal theology is caught in the
tension between conservation and commendation: this very tension is itself a stimulus to fruitful theological work.

Basic Christian claims about Jesus make ontological commit-
ments inevitable. According to the Chalcedonian definition, 'our
Lord Jesus Christ' is a single individual, 'one and the same Son'.
This one Son is said to be both 'perfect in Godhood' and 'perfect
in manhood'. The single subject is both 'one in being' (*homoousios*)
with God, 'one in being' with us, and to be 'acknowledged in two
natures'. So the catholic faith makes assumptions about human
nature and divine nature, and about the intelligibility of one individual having both. It assumes that it is possible for a subject to be
fully God and fully a human being and that in the incarnation it
actually happened. It supposes that a unity can be simultaneously a
duality and a duality simultaneously a unity. These are strikingly
ancient themes which in the course of their formulation doubtless
caused too much acrimony and division. Today, however, the difficulties engendered by honest attempts to think through these matters afresh have become a ground for abandoning altogether the
belief that Jesus is divine. But there are other less drastic ways of
proceeding which allow the ancient formulae to be a theological
resource which prompts rather than stifles imaginative
reinterpretation.

The 'person': a starting-point for Christology

Both sides of the debate about the meaning of Jesus have simply
overlooked the help that is available to them from an unexpected
quarter in the flow and counterflow of argument. Western philosophical thought since before Plato has wrestled continually with a
similar set of problems, rooted in the immediacy of human experience. The ontological problems raised by the assertion of a unity-
in-duality in Christ are matched by another set of ontological problems generated by the question 'What is a person?' Here is another
area of thought which has also tried to account for an ontological
unity-in-duality and which has been skilfully appropriated by
Christian theologians down the centuries. Some of the answers
which have been given display a remarkable structural similarity to

answers the Church has traditionally given to the question 'What is Jesus Christ?' This point can be illustrated briefly by a reference to the father of modern philosophy, Descartes.

Descartes answered the question 'What am I?' by recourse to what was, in effect, a duality-in-unity.[2] The human being, he said, is a compound of two substances: body, which occupies space, and mind, which thinks. Together they form a single individual. This answer is of course called dualism because it makes single individuals two things and one thing at the same time. According to dualists minds are unobservable, private, intangible and not in space; bodies are observable, public, tangible and in space. Yet each single person is a unity of body and mind. Already there looks to be a parallel with Christology worth pursuing. Is there not in each case an attempt made to hold together the unity of a single person while giving due emphasis to distinct attributes within the whole? But great caution is needed here and great care must be exercised in bringing the two dualisms together, not least because Cartesian dualism is generally agreed to be a profoundly unsatisfactory view of what a human being is. Reasons for rejecting Cartesian dualism are given in chapter 2. It would clearly be unwise to build into any restatement of Christian claims about Jesus a theory of persons which, while not lacking some able support,[3] has generally been discarded.

What seems to have been forgotten is that since the time of Descartes, work on the issues he took up has continued unabated, and alternatives to full-blown dualism have been taken up which, arguably, account much better for the presence of mind within the human physical organism. The subtlety and sophistication of some of these post-Cartesian analyses of the person may well provide an exciting impetus for new christological work. They are closer to the biblical understanding of the human being as an embodied being, and it will be shown in the next chapter that they provide a highly appropriate theological starting-point for an overdue exploration of the ontological issues which Christian faith in Jesus presupposes. These analyses provide Christian theology with a fresh set of conceptual tools for doing new work on the doctrine of Christ's Person. In careful hands they can help to craft the meaning of the old christological dogmas into a slimmer but more recognizable shape.

What follows is an exploration of how the Church might understand its confession of Jesus as *vere deus*, *vere homo*, truly God and truly man. It will be shown that theological reflection on the mystery of the divine Person of Christ can be greatly assisted and refined by recent work which reflects on the mystery of what it is to be a man or woman. In the opening sentence of his *In Search of Humanity* John Macquarrie says he has 'long believed that the best approach to many of the problems of theology and philosophy is through the study of our own humanity'.[4] This is the approach which will be adopted here towards Christology. New models are available to theology which have been constructed in the attempt to get our thinking as close as possible to the sort of being we ourselves are, and in a christological context these models have so far scarcely been used. A big bonus in this approach to the Person of Christ is that each of us is a person already; each of us has an immediate acquaintance with the facts and experiences which become materials out of which accounts of what persons are get constructed. Maurice Wiles has shown that theological writers, ancient and modern, have commonly assumed 'that it is in the experience of what it is to be a person that we are provided alike with the initial subject-matter and the explanatory models for our theological work'.[5] In this respect, then, nothing new is offered. In adopting an approach to the Person of Christ through the 'model' of the human person I am simply borrowing a standard method for thinking theologically. If the approach is successful, I hope to be able to show that traditional Christian teaching about Jesus can be re-presented in at least one form which avoids the evisceration of the tradition by the liberals and the defensiveness of the conservatives. The approach will be frequently contrasted with that of some of the contributors to *The Myth of God Incarnate* on the one hand, and supporters of traditional Christology on the other. The work of Jean Galot, Brian Hebblethwaite and, more recently, Thomas Morris[6] will be discussed, and an independent *via media* adopted between the liberal/radical and conservative/orthodox positions.

In what sense is the incarnation of God in Christ something that can be understood at all? There is much to be said for beginning with Wittgenstein's discussion of what happens for us to be able to say we understand something. Sometimes a person exclaims 'Now I know how to go on!', and this, says Wittgenstein, 'corresponds to an instinctive sound, a glad start'.[7] Doubt is cast on the assumption that understanding something is a matter of undergoing the appropriate set of private experiences; rather, it is something shared with others, the result of which enables us to 'go on' at the point at which we had 'got stuck'. This deceptively simple suggestion may help to show what is involved in understanding the Person of Christ. In the face of the greatest mystery of the Christian faith the most appropriate response *is* to 'get stuck'. In order to 'go on' one must first let oneself be bewildered at the sheer extravagance of the claims the Church makes about Jesus. How could a historical individual be a divine Person and a human being simultaneously? How could the timeless pre-existent Son also be the son of Joseph and Mary? To begin to understand these mind-boggling claims is to be able to say, at whatever point one is stuck, 'Now I know how to go on!' Of course one may be mistaken in thinking that one can go on. Errors and false starts all belong to getting going. But at other times one will say one knows how to go on, and be right, for ' . . . there are cases in which I should say: "When I said I knew how to go on, I *did* know." '[8] But how? Understanding the mystery of Christ is a sharing, an appropriation of that knowledge offered by the Church, the author and preserver of the ancient creeds which represent the summit of inspired human insights about the truths concerning Jesus. Since 'now we see only puzzling reflections in a mirror' (1 Corinthians 13:12),[9] there are limits to the length of the journey down the road of understanding: indeed we may not get started at all. But being *stuck* in the face of the mystery of the incarnation is the preliminary to being *struck* by it, and that is indeed a 'going on'. I hope to show that the wealth of material available which probes the mystery of what it is to be a human person can help us to 'know how to go on' when we are stuck before ontological claims about Jesus.

Analogy: an appropriate method for Christology

So the chosen method for 'going on' is analogy, the analogy between a human person and the divine/human incarnate Person of Christ. If it can be shown that there are analogies which genuinely illuminate Christian beliefs about the mystery of the incarnation of God in Christ, then any charge that that doctrine cannot be understood fails. Analogy is tricky territory to negotiate, so it is necessary to say what can, and what cannot, be gained from using it. Analogies are 'resemblances between things of different types'.[10] In Christian theology the idea of analogy is given by Aquinas a special place where it is a 'third way' of speaking about God which avoids the stark alternatives of wholly literal and wholly symbolic statements about God:

> If we are to apply creaturely terms signficantly to the Creator without degrading him to creaturely status, there must be terms applicable to creature and Creator neither *univocally* (in an identical sense) nor merely *equivocally* (in unrelated senses) but in some third way, namely *analogically* (in senses not identical, but somehow related).[11]

Despite important criticisms of analogy,[12] I accept that analogy is indispensable for speaking about God. Nonetheless there are important differences between my series of analogies between a human person and the divine Person of Christ and customary discussions about the making of analogical predications of the infinite God.

First, I claim only that analogies may illustrate, but are powerless to demonstrate, the truth or meaning of something. Analogies may elucidate, but cannot establish. Theology cannot demonstrate, by analogy or any other means, that Jesus Christ is truly God and truly man. Rather it serves the Christian Church which already holds this central belief to be true, and tries to illustrate and elucidate what is meant by it. Since analogies are tentative, exploratory and provisional, they are especially appropriate for speaking of the mystery of the being of God in Christ. They can provide genuine gains in understanding if the resemblances they pick out do genuinely provide insights into some of the things which are compared.

Second, the resemblances which form the basic series of analogies in this book are more concrete than those where, say, the goodness or wisdom of God is compared with, but greatly exceeds, the goodness and wisdom of men and women. They are more concrete because in the present case we are talking of a divine reality which 'becomes flesh' or 'was made man' and so assumes a place within the human community, where he is genuinely one of us and shares the ontological constitution which makes our human experience possible. As we shall see, it is the claim that a particular man was and is God that gives us the best available theological grounds for speaking of God analogically at all.

Six concepts of person

The danger in using analogy even in the limited illustrative sense just outlined is obvious enough. In non-theological language analogy is a comparison of like with like. In theological language the comparison is also of like with like. But where there is likeness there is also unlikeness, and in the divine case the unlikeness spans the difference between the Creator and the creature, between the infinite and finite. So it will always be necessary to say precisely what is being compared with what, and at what point the comparison breaks down. Since the series of analogies suggested in this book is grounded in the concept of a person, I shall now specify the precise treatment which this concept will receive. Borrowing two phrases from Wittgenstein, we may say the concept has 'a family of meanings' which together provide 'a complicated network of similarities'.[13] Let us now unravel some of the threads, while remembering that distinctions which are too sharp can misrepresent realities which are complex enough already. Let us say there are the following groups or families of uses: metaphysical, philosophical, psychological, moral, existential, and social.

The first or metaphysical group of uses is found in Christian Trinitarian theology and Christology.[14] The 'Person' of Christ is a divine Person; the Father and the Spirit are divine Persons. The Latin term for person is *persona*, which originally meant a party to a contract in law having rights and duties. In Roman theatre a *persona* was the role of an actor in a play, a use preserved by the heading '*dramatis personae*' which can still be found at the top of cast lists today. By the time of Christ *persona* was already in common use to mean simply an individual human being.[15] According to Boethius (d. 524) a person is 'an individual substance of rational nature'.[16] Its use in trinitarian theology helped to convey the twin convictions of the Church that God the Son and God the Spirit are also fully God, and that God is a single divine being *una substantia*, not three. None the less both Augustine and Aquinas expressed reservations about the adequacy of the term in relation to God. Persons, said Augustine, are understood

> in a mystery . . . When, then, it is asked what the three are, or who the three are, we betake ourselves to the finding out of some special or general name under which we may embrace these three; and no such name occurs to the mind, because the supereminence of the Godhead surpasses the power of customary speech.[17]

Aquinas observed that the term could not be applied to God in the same way as to creatures, but only in a more transcendent sense *'excellentiori modo'*.[18] One thoughtful commentator in the last century wrote ' . . . in relation to the Godhead the term "person" means something between (a) mere manifestation or personation, and (b) the independent, exclusive individuality of a human being'.[19]

The Greek equivalent of *persona* was *prosopon*, which in its ordinary sense originally meant 'face', 'expression', 'role' and 'individual'.[20] From the second half of the fourth century the term *hypostasis* was also used of each of the three Persons of the Trinity: 'its role was to stress the individuality of each of the three modes or forms in which the divine essence existed'.[21] A clear tension arose for orthodoxy between the stress on individuality suggested by the concept of person, and Augustine's emphasis on the relationality of the persons, each of whom are constituted by their relation to each other. In a passage in the Chalcedonian definition which will be considered in detail laer, *hypostasis* and *prosopon* appear together. Christ is acknowledged 'in two natures . . . the characteristic property of each nature being preserved, and concurring into one Person (*prosopon*) and one subsistence (*hypostasis*) . . . ' 'Person', then, is a metaphysical subject, not a human individual, and the Person of Christ is acknowledged in its divine and human natures. Much inadequate discussion about God is fed by the unfortunate confusion between modern uses of 'person' and their ancient counterparts. From now on I shall distinguish the metaphysical concept of a person from all the others by using the upper-case 'Person' for the metaphysical concept alone. The Person of the Son is the supreme divine mystery to be approached; the other concepts (philosophical, psychological, etc.) will provide the material for the human side of the analogy. The analogy will move from the ontological constitution of the human person to the ontological constitution of the divine Person of Christ. But the meta-physical concept of Person does not just appear from nowhere. It is itself the product of reflection upon the being of the human being. There is sufficient continuity between the human person and the divine Person for the exploratory analogies to be made; and there is sufficient discontinuity between them for analogies to be required if the stark alternatives between wholly literal and wholly symbolic statements about the divine Person are to be avoided.

The second group of uses is philosophical. The question 'What is a person?' has historically arisen in attempts to answer two re-lated questions, viz. 'How does one distinguish a human being from a non-human being?' and 'With what is the abiding human being to be identified?' Answers to the first question traditionally involve reference to consciousness, self-awareness, reason, thought, and so on. Locke called a 'man' a 'living organized body' like any animal, but then used the term 'person' to distinguish the human animal from other animals. His way of showing the specialness of 'person' was to claim the word stood for 'a thinking intelligent being, that has reason and reflection, and can consider itself as itself, the same thinking thing, in different times and places . . . '[22] The second question goes to the heart of the mind-body problem, and a way through it will be outlined in chapter 2.

The third or psychological group of uses of 'person' is inti-mately connected with the modern notion of 'personality', a term which has come to possess many conflicting senses. It is said that this concept of a person is 'the starting point of humanistic psy-chology . . . The "person" is the foundation of the process of development and unfolding which is revealed in character and personality.'[23] Unfortunately a standard way of speaking has de-veloped which dubiously licenses talk about a person's person-ality as if it were a sort of describable thing that is 'warm', 'cold', 'out-going', 'sullen', 'engaging', 'withdrawn', 'intense', and so on. A person's character is known through his or her behaviour, actions, remarks, beliefs, gestures, etc. The individual is not born with a character that is pre-formed. It is acquired; it grows and changes. Since this book does not draw much on psychology the psychological concept of the person appears only seldom. But talk of personality presupposes a prior philosophical concept of a person which minimally includes self-consciousness, relations with other persons, maturation and responsibility, and is an at-tempt to amplify it. We may perhaps say the value of 'personality' lies in providing a dynamic element for the philosophical con-cepts of the person.

Fourth, the moral group of uses of 'person' is indebted to Kant. His distinctions between a 'thing' and a 'person' and between 'means' and 'ends' are famous. 'Rational beings' he said, are called *persons*, because their very nature shows them to be ends in themselves, that is, something which cannot be made use of simply as a means . . . Persons are not purely subjective ends, whose existence has a value *for us* as the effect of our actions, but they are objective ends, or beings whose existence is an end in itself, for which no other end can be substituted.[24]

Persons belong in a moral community, what Kant called 'a kingdom of ends'. In acting morally we treat other persons never purely as objects or instruments for the achievement of our own purposes; instead we treat them as persons, or ends in themselves.

Fifth, modern existentialism. The term 'person' is not always found in the writings of the existentialists, yet they begin, if not with 'person', then with human existence, 'man', 'for-itself', *Dasein*, etc. Sartre held that

man first of all exists, encounters himself, surges up in the world – and defines himself afterwards. If man as the existentialist sees him is not definable, it is because to begin with he is nothing. He will not be anything until later, and then he will be what he makes of himself.

Man is 'before all else, something which propels itself towards a future and is aware that it is doing so. Man is, indeed, a project . . . '[25]

On this view, then, human existence is specifically what individuals make of themselves, and nothing else. When the term 'person' is brought into an existentialist way of thinking we may say that a person has no fixed essence or nature: he or she exists in so far as he has become what he has chosen.

The existentialist concept of a person has been rightly criticized for its narrow individuality. It should be counterbalanced, sixthly, by the social or 'communitarian' concept of a person. An individual person lives *from* others and *for* others, that is, he or she is a person-in-relation. 'Persons', wrote John Macmurray, 'are constituted by their mutual relation to one another. "I" exist only as one element in the complex "You and I".'[26] Concepts 2–6 all assume that 'person' stands for 'individual human being' while combining this minimal starting-point with other features which together provide differing and sometimes conflicting accounts of how the individual human being is to be understood. Frequent references to these different types of person-concepts will be made as the argument of the book proceeds.

The argument of the book

The purpose of the present study and the method of achieving it have both been stated, and a preliminary explanation of the 'family of meanings' which the concept of person engenders has now been made. We can now make the required connections between ancient and modern concepts of person, and between applications of the concept of person to human and divine subjects. In the next chapter that particular concept of a person which forms the basis of the 'person/Person' analogy will be set out. This is a double-aspect theory called simply 'the person theory'. Chapter 3 begins to develop a detailed analogy between the person theory and the doctrine of Christ's Person as set forth in the Chalcedonian definition. Chapter 4 explores attempts to use double or complementary languages about single entities, and it will be shown that both in the case of persons and in the case of the Person of Christ such attempts are essential. Chapter 5 establishes firm similarities between the languge used to ascribe personal characteristics to persons and the language used to ascribe divine characteristics to Jesus Christ, and the suggestion is made that christological language be understood as importantly similar to 'person language'. Our study of person language makes possible a fresh approach to the 'I am' sayings of John's Gospel, and this is attempted in chapter 6, where philosophical material will be used to support the traditional view that the 'I' which speaks with the lips of Jesus really is God-in-person.

Chapter 7 asks whether one can continue to defend the orthodox insistence that Christ, being a divine Person, lacked human personhood. Various defences of this position are shown to be lacking. It is argued that Jesus is 'truly a person, truly God', and that, contrary to appearances, such a position may be held without falling into the old 'two person' error. Chapter 8 draws on the theory of 'anomalous monism' in order to consolidate the conclusion of chapter 7 and develop some further tentative suggestions about the divine subject, God the Son. Chapter 9 then argues that the common 'whole and parts' understanding of the human person is a fruitful analogy for understanding the relation between divinity and humanity in Christ, and chapter 10 utilizes the concept of a person as a 'person-in-relation' to develop an analogy between human persons and the divine Persons of the Trinity. Chapter 11 utilizes the notion of personal knowledge in order to make suggestions about the human knowledge of God and about divine love. As the argument proceeds there is continuous engagement with conservative and liberal positions in Christology. The analogical approach adopted by the book is a *via media* between both.

NOTES

1   See, e.g., some of the contributors to John Hick (ed.), *The Myth of God Incarnate* (London: SCM Press, 1977), and Michael Goulder (ed.), *Incarnation and myth: The Debate Continued* (London: S C M Press, 1979).

2 Meditation 2. See René Descartes, *Discourse on Method and Other Writings* Harmondsworth: Penguin Classics, 1968), p. 103

3 Richard Swinburne is an influential and indefatigable supporter of substance dualism. See below pp. 14–15, and his 'The Structure of the Soul' in A. R. Peacocke and G. Gillett (eds), *Persons and Personality* (Oxford: Basil Blackwell, 1987), ch. 3, for a recent statement of his position. He takes issue with my theological criticisms of dualism in his response to my 'Christian Theism and the Concept of a Person' later in the same volume (pp. 191–2). For a longer statement, see his *The Evolution of the Soul* (Oxford: Clarendon Press, 1986).

4 John Macquarrie, *In Search of Humanity* (London: SCM Press, 1982), Preface.

5 Maurice Wiles, 'Psychological Analogies in the Fathers', *Studia Patristica*, xi (1967), pp. 264–7.

6 Jean Galot SJ, *Who is Christ? A Theology of the Incarnation* (Rome: Gregorian University Press, 1980); Brian Hebblethwaite, *The Incarnation* (Cambridge: Cambridge University Press, 1987); Thomas V. Morris, *The Logic of God Incarnate* (Ithaca and London: Cornell University Press, 1986).

7 Ludwig Wittgenstein, *Philosophical Investigations*, tr. G. E. M. Anscombe (Oxford: Basil Blackwell, 1972), i, §323.

8 ibid., author's emphasis.

9 In order to reduce footnotes and to make clearer which quotations are biblical, biblical references are maintained in the text. The New English Bible is used throughout unless otherwise stated.

10 Patrick Shaw, *Logic and its Limits* (London: Pan Books, 1981), p. 114.

11 Austin Farrer's description of Aquinas' statement of the problem of analogy. See 'Theology and Analogy 1. The Concept of Analogy' in his *Reflective Faith* (London: SPCK, 1972), p. 65.

12 Notably by Humphrey Palmer, *Analogy* (London and Basingstoke: Macmillan, 1973).

13 Wittgenstein, op. cit., §77, §66.

14 For a comprehensive analysis of 'Person', see Karl Rahner's entry 'Person' in Karl Rahner (ed.), *Encyclopaedia of Theology* (London: Burns & Oates, 2nd imp., 1977), pp. 1206–25.

15 See A. Richardson and J. Bowden (eds), *A New Dictionary of Christian Theology* (London: SCM Press, 1983), p. 442.

16 *naturae rationalis individua substantia:* Boethius, *Tractates*, tr. H. F. Stewart, E. K. Rand and S. J. Tester (London and Cambridge, Mass: William Heinemann and Harvard University Press, 1973), p. 85.

17 Augustine, *De Trinitate*, 7.4.7.

18 Thomas Aquinas, *Summa Theologiae*, 1.29.3. See R. L. Ottley, *The Doctrine of the Incarnation* (London: Methuen, ⁴1908, 1st pub. 1896), p. 572.

19 Ottley, ibid.

20 J. N. D. Kelly, *Early Christian Doctrines* (London: A. & C. Black, 1958), p. 115.

21 J. N. D. Kelly, *Early Christian Creeds* (London: A. & C. Black, ³1965), p. 241.

22 John Locke, *An Essay Concerning Human Understanding* (1960), book 2, ch. 27, §§ 8–9.

23 See H. J. Eysenck, W. Arnold and R. Meili (eds), *Encyclopaedia of Psychology* (London: Search Press, 1972), pp. 381–3.

24 I. Kant, *The Metaphysic of Morality* (1785), section 276.

25 J-P. Sartre, *Existentialism and Humanism* (London: Methuen, rep. 1978), p. 28.

26 John Macmurray, *Persons in Relation* (London: Faber & Faber, 1961), p. 24.

CHAPTER 2

The 'Person Theory': A Starting-Point for Christology

In this chapter the account of a person will be chosen which will serve as the starting-point for approaching the mystery of the divine/human Person of Christ in the rest of the book. There are three main groups of theories (and the many variations within each group must not be allowed to detain us for the moment). I first discuss Cartesian dualism and suggest that its influence on subsequent philosophical and religious thought has been unfortunate. I argue next that the rival materialist group of theories is reductionist and does not present a satisfactory alternative to dualism. Then the 'person theory' is outlined and defended as a viable alternative to both dualism and materialism. This is the theory which begins the analogy between the human person and the divine Person in chapter 3. The philosophical analysis of the present chapter may not be wholly congenial to readers who are keen to plunge into the christological issues straightaway, but the philosophical work has to be done, and their patience will soon be rewarded.

The tradition of dualism

The tradition of dualism in the West goes back to Plato, who taught the complete separability of the soul from the body, identifying the thinking, reasonable person with his or her soul, and regarding the death of the body as the soul's eternal release.[1] But the *locus classicus* for mind/body dualism in the modern period is Descartes. According to Descartes a human being is a compound of two substances, a 'thinking thing' (*res cogitans*) and an 'extended thing' (*res extensa*). The thinking thing or mind is the essential self, the principle of personal identity. 'I am therefore, precisely speaking, only a thing which thinks, that is to say, a mind, understanding, or reason . . . '[2] Once the two substances are separated the physical substance is relegated to an inferior order of being. The body is blamed for leading the mind into error by presenting it with misleading ideas which derive from the senses. 'It is possible that all those images, and, in general, all the things one relates to the nature of body, are nothing but dreams or chimera.'[3] The body is even dispensable altogether, being inessential to the existence of the self. 'It is certain that I, that is to say my mind, by which I am what I am, is entirely and truly distinct from my body, and may exist without it.'[4] Bodies lack consciousness and self-awareness. They are, like machines,[5] subject to the laws of nature.

A dualistic model of a person will not be used in our approach to the Person of Christ. I join the large consensus of writers, from Hobbes, Fr Arnauld and Princess Elizabeth, who were contemporaries of Descartes, to some of the influential figures of twentieth-century philosophy, e.g. Russell, Heidegger, Ryle, Wittgenstein, Strawson and Rorty, in thinking the problems for dualism are insurmountable. While they disagree about much else, they hold dualism to be seriously mistaken. But dualism is still influential,[6] and probably still deserves to be called the 'official doctrine', as Ryle sarcastically dubbed it.[7] It has shaped subsequent discussion of such diverse philosophical problems as the nature of knowledge, consciousness, personal identity and will, as well as action, freedom, and like matters. The abiding importance of dualism lies in its refusal to allow that the developed conscious states which only persons have are just physical states. But once Descartes' question 'Who am I?' is allowed to suggest an answer which brings into use the idea of separate mental and physical substances, dualism cannot show, it can only assert, that what corresponds to the pronoun 'I' is really something mental.[8] Having answered his question with separate substances Descartes was unable subsequently to unify them. The price he pays for discarding the body in the endeavour to identify the essential self as a mind is his later inability to reintegrate the excluded body with the unembodied mind. His final 'Meditation' leaves him weakly positing a second doctrine of the self, one 'composed of body and mind'.[9] But the principle of the union of body and mind is unresolved; so too is the relation between the two 'I's, the unembodied and the embodied.

At the very least supporters of dualism have additionally to provide some account of an entity which is not in space and so not locatable within the body; of how it interacts reciprocally with its body; of why it is so influenced by its body if it is really independent of it; and of how it is possible for a person to be a unity given the distinct and separate substances he or she must embrace. Some modern critics (a number of whom are discussed later) have rightly pointed to mistakes made by dualists in supposing that words like 'mind', 'will' and 'intellect' name an 'inner' substance or substances, while others have shown that Cartesianism isolates individuals from each other and ignores the social character of persons and the language we inherit from them, even in describing ourselves. For these reasons I think there is a strong case against dualism being true.

It is important to consider some of the unfortunate consequences of dualism,[10] even if Descartes did not intend them.

Thinking comes to be elevated above all other human accomplish-
ments and experiences – the human being is literally 'a thinking
thing'. The spiritual life, which might in Christian theology be
assessed by its openness to God and to other people, becomes an
enclosed, private and intellectual affair. The human body is easily
disparaged as inessential to the mind and to personal identity.
Since only minds are conscious, the body is no more than an
object, a machine governed by mechanical laws. Deprived of its
soul, it ceases to have religious significance. It may even be understood as inherently evil, set against the spirit, and having no part,
even in a reconstituted form, in any post-mortem existence which a
loving God may choose to confer. It is hard to see how Descartes'
anti-physical prejudices can be squared with the Christian doctrines of creation and resurrection.[11] Other people have no part in
establishing one's self-identity or self-certainty. Descartes' famous
proof of his own existence, the *cogito ergo sum*, is conducted without
help, alone. Relationships with other people feature nowhere in his
ontology. Our feelings and emotions, essential ingredients of our
moral and aesthetic awareness, are untrustworthy because of their
bodily origins and are of no philosophical interest. A sad bifurca-
tion of our being is allowed to disrupt the unity a person essentially
is.

Monism, then, is a provisional choice over against dualism in
human ontology. But Richard Swinburne has recently put forward
two further arguments for dualism, one based on the alleged inability of opponents to account for the person in his or her totality.
He defines the person as 'the soul together with whatever, if any,
body is linked temporarily to it', and holds that non-dualists cannot account for a person's continuing conscious life without referring to the soul. The second argument is based on the logical
possibility 'that persons continue to exist when their bodies are
destroyed'. 'The most natural way of making sense of this fact',
continues Swinburne, is to talk of 'persons as consisting of two
parts, body and soul – the soul being the essential part, whose
continuing alone makes for the continuing of the person'.[12]

Both arguments are supported by thought experiments. If one of
the hemispheres of a brain were removed from a person and trans-
planted into the skull of a living body from which the brain had
been removed, 'there would then appear to be two separate living
persons'.[13] While we would know what had happened to the parts
of a person's body, we would not know what had happened to the
person. Further thought experiments follow which purport to show
that a person can continue to exist disembodied. It is plausible to
imagine a man losing control of his own body while gaining control
of his wife's body; if he can imagine this he can imagine losing
control of his own body while continuing to exist disembodied,

remaining the subject of whatever mental life he continues to have.[14] It is thus logically possible to exist unembodied, and we can see the good sense of this possibility 'if we think of a person as body plus soul, such that the continuing of the soul alone guarantees the continuing of the person'.[15]

Both these arguments are unconvincing. We might well wonder just what weight is being placed on thought-experiments as the argument proceeds, and how legitimate they are generally in the course of establishing conclusions. In this particular case we might wonder how plausible the imagined case of a split-brain transplant is, how the survival of the separate hemispheres apart from each other and their former body is possible, how one hemisphere could be surgically connected up with the organs and nervous system of its new host body, and so on. These real difficulties are in danger of turning the thought-experiments into fantasies. But supporters of thought-experiments will be unmoved by practical objections, for (they will say) they are intended only to illustrate possibilities. Well then, let us grant the possibility of a split-brain transplant – now the argument can begin about what follows from it. All that can be inferred from the experiment is that there would be a few bizarre people whose identity would be a puzzle to themselves and to others, for reasons that would be well understood. Such people would not entitle us to come to particular conclusions about the constitution of everyone.

There are other problems with Swinburne's arguments. The point might be granted (though it need not be) that I can imagine existing in someone else's body or without my body, but it doesn't follow from my alleged ability to imagine something that it is a possibility.[16] Alternatively, if it is logically possible that I can exist without my body, it does not follow that it will come about any more than the logical possibility of a world without dogs or cats will come about. More important a set of very challengeable dualistic assumptions is written into the experiments in the first place, that 'I' am separate from my body, that my soul is what makes me me, that the subject of our 'mental life' is non-physical, and so on. But non-dualists challenge these assumptions, and that is what the argument is about. It is also unclear how dualists would themselves handle the dilemmas introduced by the split-brain experiment. For these reasons recent defences of dualism may be no more convincing than earlier ones. There is no need for Christians to think that their hope in the life everlasting depends on the notion of a substantial soul.[17]

Monism and materialism

Monism, then, is to be preferred to dualism. A person is a single substance. But there are different types of monism and some of them are almost as unsatisfactory as the dualism they replace. The view that persons are, without remainder, bodies is variously called materialism, physicalism, or the mind/brain identity theory. One recent materialist has typically worked out 'an account of the nature of mind which is compatible with the view that man is nothing but a physico-chemical mechanism'.[18] Materialism has great attractions. For example, it appears simpler than dualism. Since the mind is to be identified with the brain (or the brain and the central nervous system), and a person is to be identified with his or her body *tout court*, whatever states persons undergo are physical states. Consequently all the problems connected with the interaction between mind and brain, or consciousness and the body, vanish. All interactions are physical and take place within the unity of the physical organism.

This approach to the person, like the dualism it replaces, cannot help us either. It lays to rest the Cartesian 'ghost in the machine' but at too heavy a price. Descartes' ontology at least made room in the world for minds as well as machines. The ontology of materialism leaves us with only machines. While dualism splits the unity of the person, materialism can be accused of removing persons from the world altogether. At any rate the concept of a person undergoes a drastic change. The main objection which a mind/brain identity theory has to face is a logical one. If the claim is made that two or more objects or events are identical with each other, there must already be some similarity of genus, class, category, etc. which makes possible the claim that they are the same. Let us say that cars and bicycles belong to the same genus (means of transport), but they belong to different classes, one with four wheels, one with only two, and so on. Now, my car might be the same make as my friend's, but if my friend owns only a bicycle, then, while we have items in the same genus, the claim that we have the same make of car could not even be advanced. Cars and bicycles belong to different classes. Claims about thoughts (which are mental) and brain-processes (which are physical) seem unable to avoid this logical difficulty. Whatever a neuro-surgeon may observe going on in a patient's brain, and however justified he or she may be in correlating what is happening with the patient's reports of what is happening, the accounts given by each of them, one in terms of the behaviour of synapses, sub-systems, and so on, the other in terms of sensations, thoughts, desires, and so on, are of a different logical sort. The experience of a thought and the observation of a brain-process are events of two different orders. No neuro-surgeon is going to observe a thought in the brain, whatever else may be happening. To speak of thoughts and feelings by means of words like 'events' and 'processes' is already to fall into misdescription. If one does this, one uses observation-language to describe something that cannot be observed.[19]

So materialism seems unable to account for the character of human consciousness within the human organism. Work on human brains which localizes separate mental functions such as emotion, memory and motor control[20] provides impressive evidence for a correlation between neural happenings and mental happenings, but it can never be evidence for identity between them. A consequence of mis-identifying conscious mental states with material states is inevitably reductionism, leading to determinism and behaviourism. 'Reductionism' occurs whenever the complex is insufficiently explained by means of the simple; the most obvious examples are those frequent cases where human conduct is apparently 'explained' by comparison with that of animals. The inadequacy of reductive accounts of human activities can be demonstrated by a consideration of any of the things which persons do and non-persons do not do, like listening to music and enjoying it. A sufficient description (i.e. one that is adequate to what is being explained) of listening to Shostakovich and enjoying it cannot be given in terms of sound waves, auditory nerves, neurochemical changes in the brain, etc. Such things will be necessary for the experience to occur and will be among the necessary but not sufficient conditions for its occurrence. But on the personal level a physical description will be uninteresting, for the person who enjoys Shostakovich is likely to give reasons for his or her enjoyment which are just not cashable in physical terms. This is because there is more taking place in the single activity of enjoying listening to Shostakovich than physical descriptions can ever satisfy. As soon as reductive descriptions of persons and their actions are treated as sufficient, the means for challenging the various shifting orthodoxies of behaviourism, determinism and positivism are disallowed.

A similar kind of reductionism has a history in Christology too, though the parallels have not generally been noticed. Unitarian Christians do for the Person of Christ what materialists do for persons. Faced with the complexity of him who was both 'truly God and truly man',[21] Unitarians remove half the problem by removing half the complexity. The necessary truth that Jesus of Nazareth is a human being becomes the sufficient truth as well – Jesus of Nazareth is *only* a human being, nothing more. Recent theological liberalism makes a similar mistake. Don Cupitt has argued that the logical difficulties involved in saying, as Christians do, that 'Jesus is God' are overwhelming. Because the name 'Jesus' refers to a historical individual, Jesus cannot then be identical with God in any of the meanings Cupitt assigns to the word 'God'.[22] Confronted with this apparently insuperable difficulty, his solution is to abandon the historic faith of the Church completely (as the title of his subsequent book *Taking Leave of God* indicates).

Instead of the incarnational faith, 'Jesus, in short, was a prophet who brought the tradition of prophetic monotheism to completion.'[23] A necessary description becomes a sufficient one. Because Jesus was this, Jesus was *only* this. As we shall see, a wiser course of action would have been to look about for precedents where apparently incompatible predicates do belong to the same individual. A precedent could have been found in the reality which every person is, and Cupitt's reduction of incarnational faith avoided. I shall attempt to show that the mystery which is the human person is also the clue to the greater mystery which is the Person of the divine Son (chapter 3).

Materialism reduces all phenomena to material phenomena. Another kind of reduction is idealism, where all material phenomena are reduced to mental phenomena. What exists is either minds or ideas. Most writers today agree with Hylas (the character in Bishop Berkeley's dialogue) that idealism is 'the most extravagant opinion that ever entered into the mind of man, to wit, that there is no such thing as *material substance* in the world',[24] so it will not be pursued. But one can hardly refrain from comparing idealism with the tendency in Christian thought and culture known as docetism. Idealism holds that matter is apparent but not real; docetism holds that our Lord's humanity is apparent but not real. Both views deny material substances. Both views represent an extreme reaction to ontological complexity. Neither can tolerate a world with some dualism in it, whether minds and bodies or divinity and humanity. So half of the dualism is excised. Materialism lives without minds; idealism without bodies. Unitarianism jettisons our Lord's divinity; docetism affirms nothing else.

The double-aspect theory

So substantive dualism can be ruled out as an adequate account of what persons are and the apparently simpler monist alternatives turn out to be reductive. Against this background double-aspect theories of persons are welcome and attractive. Despite the initial unpromisingness of 'aspect' (a spatial metaphor suggesting that the mental and the physical can be viewed) double-aspect theories assume that a person is a unitary self which necessarily gives rise to double descriptions or predicates which correspond to the twin properties of persons as embodied and capable of thought. Spinoza propounded this type of theory, holding that 'Mind and body are one and the same thing, conceived first under the attribute of thought, secondly, under the attribute of extension.'[25] This type of theory is widely held,[26] and the most sophisticated and discussed version of it is P. F. Strawson's, usually called the 'person theory' because of his use of the concept 'person' in chapter 3 of his *Individuals*.

Strawson's definition of a person looks at first to be difficult; in fact it is profoundly simple. He rejects both dualism and materialism while retaining essential elements of both. Against dualism he will not allow that a person is a combination of substances; against materialism he will not allow that a person is a material substance only. Those are the disagreements. But he agrees with materialism that a person is one substance. And he agrees with dualism that the reality of conscious mental states cannot be reduced to physical states. So a person is a unity-in-duality. That is why he defines the concept of a person as 'the concept of a type of entity such that *both* predicates ascribing states of consciousness *and* predicates ascribing corporeal characteristics, a physical situation, etc. are equally applicable to a single individual of that single type'.[27] This careful definition is the result of the attempt to show that the traditional argument between dualism and monism presupposes an unacknowledged view of what a person is before the debate gets going. Both mental states and physical states are abstracted from a personal reality which is prior both in thought and in fact. The concept of a person, says Strawson, is 'logically prior to that of an individual consciousness. The concept of a person is not to be analysed as that of an animated body or of an embodied anima.'[28]

There are important gains to be had from putting the matter in this way. They have been much discussed among philosophers of mind, and it cannot be helped if these discussions are not yet well known among theologians. Briefly put, the main change between Cartesian dualism and the 'person theory' is a move from thinking of persons as two things or substances which are somehow united, to thinking of them as one thing or substance which must be looked at from two different aspects. Cartesian dualism, then, is a substance or 'substantive' dualism. The move to the person theory is a move from 'substantive' dualism to substantive monism. A person is one thing, not two. This fact will be most important when building an analogy which illustrates the unity of the one divine Person of Christ. But although the person theory is monistic with respect to the number of substances a person is, it is not monistic in the way materialism is. That is because the complexity of the person requires two perspectives, or 'double-aspects', to account for it. This is called 'attribute' or 'attributive' dualism. Attributive dualism will greatly assist in the building of the analogy which illustrates the two natures of the one Christ.

The 'person theory' is examined more closely when its possibilities for building analogies from the human person to the divine Person are spelled out in chapter 3. Let us consider now some further philosophical reasons for preferring it to either substantive dualism or substantive materialism. The careful definition of the person short-circuits Cartesian dualism by showing that the unity

of the person underlies any separation of mental and physical
states. Strawson rightly insists that 'a necessary condition of states
of consciousness being ascribed at all is that they should be ascribed to the *very same things* as certain corporeal characteristics, a
certain physical situation, etc.' Thoughts then cannot just be ascribed to minds. They must be ascribed to beings which also have
bodies. We are to resist the temptation, he continues, 'to think of a
person as a sort of compound of two kinds of subjects: a subject of
experiences (a pure consciousness, an ego) on the one hand, and a
subject of corporeal attributes on the other. Many questions arise
when we think in this way.' New logical rules for the concept of
person are provided by Strawson which stress its primitiveness and
show that the idea of separate mental states derives from it. By
speaking of the concept of person as 'primitive', attention is drawn
to the basic unity of personal experience which one has prior to
philosophical reflection upon consciousness or upon the nature of
the person.

If the whole person be accepted as the basic starting-point for
reflection on mental and physical states alike, important philosophical consequences follow. It now becomes difficult to advance any
theory about persons on the basis of separate mental or physical
states without breaking the new rules which govern this basic concept of person. Both materialists and dualists are likely to start with
a notion of a subject of mental states which is logically separable
from their notion of a material body. The former then goes on to
say that in fact the subject of mental states is identical with some
material body; the latter goes on to say that the subject of mental
states is a separate substance distinct from the body. But the isola-
tion of the notion of a subject of mental states from the notion of a
person in the first place is rightly challenged by the person theory
and exposed as a move which writes dualism into the account,
instead of providing an argument for it. A conceptual veto is successfully placed on attempts to identify a logical subject of consciousness while at the same time excluding that subject's essential
materiality. And this conceptual veto protects the ontological unity
of the person.[29]

So the person theory seems to provide an ontological monism
with regard to human beings while avoiding the difficulties which
dualism and materialism run into. Against the mind/brain identity
theory, it requires no statement of identity between logically different substances or states, for it acknowledges the logical differences between them. It does not make the mistake of trying to
establish a conceptual conclusion by an appeal to empirical premises: it is happily consistent with the view that our personal and
mental experiences have a complex physical basis. And it avoids
the danger of reductionism whereby physical states are the sole

states for organisms to be in. Against dualism it does not assert that the real existence of the person is mental. It avoids the fatal split within the unity of the individual, and it avoids an unfortunate practical consequence of dualism, viz. the frequent relegation of the body to an inferior status in comparison with the mind.

The person theory will form the basis of a series which moves from the being of the human person to the being of the divine Person of Christ. By this point I hope to have shown in sufficient detail why it is to be preferred to both dualism and materialism. But while theologians may tire at the minutiae of philosophical discussion, philosophers are likely to think that there are as many problems with double-aspect theories as with their rivals. For this reason, some further treatment of the philosophical objections is given in an extended note.[30]

The person theory occupies the middle ground between dualism and materialism. It remains to be noted that the theory is fully consistent with biblical accounts of human nature, and that it stands closer to the thought of Aristotle and Aquinas than its dualistic counterpart. We may recall the words of Henry Wheeler Robinson, often quoted in this connection, that

> Over against the Greek idea of an immortal soul temporarily inhabiting an earthly body, the Hebrew psychology gives us not an incarnated soul, but an animated body, as its characteristic doctrine of resurrection clearly shows, and this doctrine has proved able to maintain itself in its Pauline transformation, as the basis of the hope of the future.[31]

It is a standard view among modern theologians that a person is an 'embodied self'[32] or a unity 'logically and objectively prior' to the distinguishable elements of matter and spirit.[33]

For Aristotle the soul is the form of the body, that by which a body potentially has life.[34] He emphatically rejects the view that soul and body are two things. One recent commentator sees Aristotle's theory of soul and body as anticipating the more modern idea that there can be 'two levels of description of a single thing's history'.[35] (The idea of complementary descriptions is taken up in chapters 4 and 5.) Aquinas' account of the soul is heavily dependent on Aristotle, and he too denies that the soul is a separate substance. In his discussion of the nature of the soul in the *Summa Theologiae*, Aquinas denies that the soul can be called a hypostasis or person, for, on his view, this would wrongly name the person by one of its parts, like the hand or foot.[36] The soul, he says, is 'the form of the human body', and the soul understood as intellect is the form of the thinking man. The statement 'Socrates understands', urges Aquinas, cannot be rendered 'the intellect of Socrates understands', for understanding is ascribed not to the intellect but to Socrates as a man. It is 'predicated of him essentially'.[37] The suggestion that the soul is separate from but linked to the body is rejected, 'because this link or union does not sufficiently explain that the act of the intellect is the act of Socrates'. 'There remains, therefore, no other explanation', continues Aquinas, 'than that given by Aristotle – namely, that this particular man understands because the intellectual principle is his form.'[38]

The person theory, then, provides a 'model' of a person which is consistent with biblical thought, is closer than dualism to the thought of Aristotle and Aquinas, and is also in common theological use. What is new is the attempt to explore what it is for Jesus Christ to be a Person of God, taking our cues from what it is for us to be human persons. This task leads us to ontology, and to a theory of persons which already appears in some modern versions of 'the doctrine of man' (as it is still often called). Strawson's 'person theory' is a useful starting-point (though only a starting-point) for the task. For, as the next chapter indicates, both the person theory and the Chalcedonian definition of the Person of Christ are about individuals who, while remaining essential unities, necessarily give rise to two distinct yet complementary languages.

NOTES

1 Plato, *Alcibiades* 1, 129b–130c; *Phaedo*, 64b–118.
2 René Descartes, Meditation 2 (1641), in *Discourse on Method and Other Writings* (Harmondsworth: Penguin Books, 1968), p. 105.
3 ibid., p. 106.
4 ibid., p. 156.
5 ibid., p. 163.
6 H. D. Lewis was a lifelong defender of dualism. See, e.g., his *The Elusive Mind* (London: Allen & Unwin, 1969). Richard Swinburne is the most formidable current defender of dualism. See, e.g., Sydney Shoemaker and Richard Swinburne, *Personal Identity* (Oxford: Basil Blackwell, 1984); 'The Structure of the Soul' in A. R. Peacocke and G. Gillett (eds), *Persons and Personality* (Oxford: Basil Blackwell, 1987); and *The Evolution of the Soul* (Oxford: Clarendon Press), 1986.
7 Gilbert Ryle, *The Concept of Mind* (Harmondsworth: Penguin Books, 1976, 1st pub. 1949), p. 13.
8 G. N. A. Vesey (ed.). *Body and Mind* (London: Allen & Unwin, 1964), p. 36.
9 Descartes, op. cit., p. 160.
10 Hans Küng, *Does God Exist?* (London and New York: Collins & Doubleday, 1980), pp. 26–41.
11 See my 'Christian Theism and the Concept of a Person' in Peacocke and Gillett (eds), *Persons and Personality*, pp. 183–5.
12 Swinburne, *The Evolution of the Soul*, pp. 146–7.
13 ibid., p. 148.
14 ibid., pp. 151–2.
15 ibid., p. 160.
16 See my 'The Personal God and a God who is a Person', *Religious Studies*, xxi, (1985), pp. 65–6.
17 Thatcher, 'Christian Theism and the Concept of a Person', p. 184.
18 D. M. Armstrong, *The Nature of Mind and Other Essays* (Brighton: Harvester Press, 1981), p. 2.

19 See L. Wittgenstein, *Philosophical Investigations* (Oxford: Basil Blackwell, 1972, 1st pub. 1953), §308.

20 See Edgar Wilson, *The Mental as Physical* (London: Routledge & Kegan Paul, 1979), pp. 56–7.

21 Irenaeus, *Adv. haer.*, 4.6.7.

22 Don Cupitt, 'Jesus and the Meaning of "God" ' in Michael Goulder (ed.), *Incarnation and Myth: The Debate Continued* (London: SCM Press, 1979), p. 31.

23 ibid., p. 39.

24 George Berkeley, *Three Dialogues between Hylas and Philonous*, 1 (1713) in *The Principles of Human Knowledge with Other Writings* (London and Glasgow: Collins, 1962), p. 150.

25 Spinoza, *Ethics* (1677), part 3, proposition 2: cit. Antony Flew (ed.), *Body, Mind and Death* (Macmillan: New York, 1964), p. 146.

26 G. H. Lewes, A. Bain, H. Spencer, C. S. Sherrington and D. M. MacKay held, or hold, versions of it. See G. N. A. Vesey, *The Embodied Mind* (London: Allen & Unwin, 1965), p. 24.

27 P. F. Strawson, *Individuals* (London: Methuen, 1959), pp. 101–2.

28 ibid., p. 103.

29 The person theory accords well with the later Wittgenstein's use of the term 'human being'. Wittgenstein cryptically remarks ' – It comes to this: only of a living human being and what resembles (behaves like) a living human being can one say: it has sensations; it sees; is blind; hears; is deaf; is conscious or unconscious' *Philosophical Investigations*, §281). The remark draws our attention to unavoidable assumptions we have to make about other human beings in order to be able to ascribe appropriate properties either to them, from whom we learned our language, or to ourselves.

30 Among the objections are: i) that Strawson's concept of a person is technical, and has nothing to do with how we talk about people, or how people enter relationships with each other (D. W. Hamlyn, *Metaphysics* (Cambridge: Cambridge University Press, 1984), pp. 193, 202); ii) that the shift from a dualism of substances to a dualism of descriptions only masks the opaqueness of the alleged single subject of the descriptions ('two descriptions of *what?*') (see Richard Rorty, *Philosophy and the Mirror of Nature* (Oxford: Basil Blackwell, 1980), p. 18); a person just becomes a philosophical puzzle, something neither wholly physical nor wholly mental (e. g. Jerome Shaffer, *Philosophy of Mind* (Englewood Cliffs: Prentice-Hall, 1968), p. 56; iii) the concept of a person is not logically primitive, for states of consciousness need not be ascribed to the same thing as corporeal characteristics (Hamlyn, *Metaphysics*, p. 200); iv) that if, as Strawson claims, I ascribe states of consciousness to myself I must already be able to ascribe states of consciousness to others, I thus lack any principle or criteria for identifying my experiences as *mine* (A. J. Ayer, 'The Concept of a Person' in *The Concept of a Person and Other Essays* (London and Basingstoke: Macmillan, 1963), p. 89; and v) Strawson's concept of a person does not explain the relation between material and mental properties by claiming that a single subject has both (A. J. Ayer, *Philosophy in the Twentieth Century* (London: Counterpoint, Unwin Paperbacks), pp. 179–90.

In reply, it may be conceded i) that Strawson's concept owes little to ordinary language use and does not tell us much about people in their relationships. But the concept belongs to a level of analysis which other levels presuppose. Strawson's concept, in terms of the sixfold catalogue of uses of 'person' developed in chapter 1, is a *philosophical* concept. The psychological and social uses of 'person' derive from, and thus presuppose, the ontologically prior level of analysis in which Strawson engages. ii) Rorty's dismissal of 'neo-dualism' is part of a larger project of dissolving many of the traditional problems of philosophy, and even if he is partially successful about this, I think the relationship between conscious states and physical states will rightly continue to attract philosophical attention. Theologians may justly point to that tradition of philosophy, from Kant through existentialism to the present day, which regards persons as importantly unanalysable, open, transcendent and free. People, we may say, are alone among created beings in their freedom, at least to some extent, to become what they choose, to assume responsibility for their actions, etc. The fact that Strawson's person is 'more than' a body while not being a pure consciousness or ego I welcome as an added attraction (and develop in subsequent chapters), and claim that contemporary accounts of matter give us a much expanded concept of 'body'. iii) Hamlyn's point is that while P-predicates should not *necessarily* be ascribed to beings with corporeal characteristics, there is no objection to them normally being contingently ascribed. They are contingent since they are ascribed to self and others on the basis of behaviour. Since, in order to provide an example of ascribing P-predicates to some being with no M-predicates we have to evoke spirits or angels (who says they have no bodies?) or God, Strawson's concept remains secure. iv) The problem of identifying which states are mine and which are someone else's arises in a particular philosophical context, viz. the 'no ownership theory of the self' and the other minds problem. The sense in which my toothache is mine, and not, say, my readers', is clear enough even if talk of 'ownership' of aches is problematic and the subject of such states is not yet clarified. v) The relation between material and mental properties may not be explained by means of the concept of the person, but the concept of the person does not have to be understood primarily as an attempt to provide an explanation of this relation. Rather, it provides an account of the human being which takes for granted our materiality without reducing mental states to physical states. Perhaps, as Bernard Williams suggests, the facts of consciousness cannot be explained at all (B. Williams, *Descartes, The Project of Pure Enquiry* (Harmondsworth: Penguin Books, 1987), p. 295.) This suggestion is taken up in chapter 8.

I remain convinced of the adequacy of the person theory, though any theory is likely to have defects. I am not required to establish the complete triumph of the theory over against its rivals; indeed I shall have reason to supplement it as the argument proceeds. I am required to show that it is a defensible position from which to begin the planned series of analogies, and hope by now to have done so.

31 Henry Wheeler Robinson, *The Christian Experience of the Holy Spirit* (London and Glasgow: Collins Fontana, 1962, 1st pub. 1928), p. 29.

32 John Macquarrie, *Principles of Christian Theology* (London: S C M Press, 1966), p. 65.

33 Karl Rahner, *Theological Investigations*, *Vol. 5* (London: Darton, Longman & Todd, 1966), pp. 161–2.

34 Aristotle, *De Anima*, 2.

35 J. L. Ackrill, *Aristotle the Philosopher* (Oxford: Oxford University Press, 1981), p. 76.

36 Aquinas, *Summa Theologica*, Question 75, art. 4.

37 ibid., Question 76, art. 1.

38 ibid.

CHAPTER 3

Persons – Human and Divine

In this chapter a detailed comparison is undertaken between the concept of the person in the person theory and the concept of the divine Person of Christ in the statement agreed by the fathers at the Council of Chalcedon in 451. Basic common structural features of the two concepts are noted, and further exploration yields up parallel logical rules governing the use of each, which are then compared and developed. The verdict is that, despite obvious dissimilarities, there remains sufficient in common between the two person concepts for the analogy to be taken further.

The union of soul and body

There is ample precedent in the ancient literature for the drawing of comparisons between the ontological unity of soul and body in the individual person and the ontological unity of the divine and the human in the Person of Christ. Augustine (d.430) used the unity of body and soul in the human person in order to explain to the pagan Volusian how God and man had become one in the Person of Christ.[1] And Cyril of Alexandria (d.444), to take just one more example, compared the indwelling of the divine Word in flesh with 'such an indwelling as the soul of man may be said to have with its own body'. 'We do not distribute the Words of our Saviour in the Gospels to two several subsistences or Persons', he continues. 'For the one and sole Christ is not twofold, although we conceive of him as consisting of two distinct elements inseparably united, *even as a man is conceived of as consisting of soul and body, and yet is not twofold but one out of both.*'[2] Cyril understood the union of soul and body in a Platonic way but he none the less insisted on the indivisible unity of both in the one (human) person. Indeed this unity was essential in his bitter argument with Nestorius about the latter's alleged separation of the divine and human natures in Christ. Cyril's Platonism will not be adopted here, but his assumption that the ontology of a person helps us to understand the ontology of the Person of Christ is a valuable one which I shall borrow. Any claims on the theological side of the comparison do not derive from claims on the philosophical side. They are made on the basis of the tradition about Christ which is there already. And that tradition actively invites comparisons of this kind to be made.

It is necessary to rule out early on some possible misunderstand-ings which these comparisons might suggest. One of the basic problems occupying the minds of fourth-century theologians was whether, in Christ, the Word merely took flesh, or whether the Word took a complete humanity, comprising body and soul.[3] The former of these alternatives, the 'Word-flesh' Christology, implied no more than that the divine Word took a human body. The hu-man soul of Jesus then becomes problematic. Athanasius (d. 373) had difficulty in affirming the human soul of Jesus and so his real human psychology.[4] In the thought of Apollinarius (d.390) the Word replaces the soul of Jesus altogether. The unity between the Word and flesh is emphasized; the price to be paid is the removal of part of the humanity, a solution rejected by the Church. According to the second alternative, the 'Word-man' (*logos-anthropos*) Christology, the Word takes a complete 'man'. There is a unity between God and man in Christ, and the manhood is already a unity of body and soul. The human psychology of Jesus is affirmed but not his independent human personality, for Jesus is one Per-son, not two.

Those who in the ancient Church advocated that Jesus had no human psychology also used the body/soul unity in the human person as a basis for their one-sided (and heretical) view of Jesus,[5] and it is appropriate now to scotch any reappearance of the Apollinarian error as our modern series of personal analogies be-gins to unfold. The soul on the human side of the analogy could be made to stand for the Logos on the christological side with the obvious result that God is united not to a complete human being but to a human body. In this book, by contrast, the analogies in the series which is about to begin are non-dualist and emphasize the unity of the human person where body and soul are separable in thought but not in reality. A major emphasis in the book (chapter 7) is the extent to which it is possible to affirm the real human personhood of Jesus. The unity which the human person already is provides the analogical material for reverent speculation about that new unity, the divine/human Person of Christ. While the term 'incarnation' is retained, it is assumed throughout that Jesus was really and completely man in body and soul.

The person theory and the Chalcedonian definition

The Chalcedonian definition will be used as an authoritative state-ment of what the Church believes about Jesus Christ. As several clauses of the definition will be examined in what follows, it is reproduced here in full:

> Wherefore, following the holy Fathers, we all with one voice confess our Lord Jesus Christ one and the same Son, the same perfect in Godhead, the same perfect in manhood, truly God and truly man, the same consis-

ting of a reasonable soul and a body, of one substance with the Father as touching the Godhead, the same of one substance with us as touching the manhood, like us in all things apart from sin; begotten of the Father before the ages as touching the Godhead, the same in the last days, for us and for our salvation, born from the Virgin Mary, the *Theotocos*, as touching the manhood, one and the same Christ, Son, Lord, Only-begotten, to be acknowledged in two natures, without confusion, without change, without division, without separation; the distinction of natures being in no way abolished because of the union, but rather the characteristic property of each nature being preserved, and concurring into one Person and one subsistence, not as if Christ were parted or divided into two persons, but one and the same Son and only-begotten God, Word, Lord, Jesus Christ; even as the Prophets from the beginning spoke concerning him, and our Lord Jesus Christ instructed us, and the Creed of the Fathers has handed down to us.[6]

Let us first simply notice some remarkable structural similarities between the ontological unity-in-duality expressed by the definition and the ontological unity-in-duality expressed by the person theory in the last chapter. At this stage of the argument the similarities are merely being pointed out. They are just there, waiting to be noticed. Here are three. First, the Person of Christ, as he is described in the definition, is emphatically a single entity. 'Our Lord Jesus Christ' is 'one and the same Son', 'one and the same Christ, Son, Lord, Only-begotten'. Christ's two distinct natures are united in 'one Person and one subsistence'. The frequent repetition of the phrase 'the same' shows, according to R. V. Sellers, 'that the doctrine under discussion was not so much that of Christ's natures as that of the *unity of his Person* . . . the fundamental truth that he who was eternally with the Father is he who became man'.[7] Second, the idea that Christ is, or is comprised of, two substances or Persons is deliberately excluded. Any duality of substance is ruled out, 'not as if Christ were parted or divided into two persons', and he is reaffirmed as 'one and the same Son and only-begotten God, Word, Lord, Jesus Christ'. Third (borrowing a familiar term from the philosophy of mind), 'double aspects' upon the one Christ are essential if his identity is to be understood. These double aspects are of course his divinity and humanity, and they are subtly interwoven in the text of the definition. On the one hand he is 'perfect in Godhead', 'truly God', 'of one substance with the Father', 'begotten of the Father'; on the other hand he is 'perfect in manhood', 'truly man', 'of one substance with us', and 'born from the Virgin Mary'.

Remarkably, these features of the Chalcedonian definition of Christ's Person have their parallels in Strawson's definition of the person. Human persons are also single entities prior to any attempt to separate them into distinct substances (consciousness and corporeality). They cannot be identified with either minds apart from bodies or bodies apart from minds, because the inclusive, single concept of the person is logically prior to any dualistic division of it. So the idea that a person is, or is comprised of, two substances is excluded. And double aspects upon the one person are again essential in order to give appropriate weight to the distinctiveness which persons possess among all other 'individuals'. In each case, the Person and the person, it becomes necessary to speak of logically irreducible subjects giving rise to double sets of predicates which are both distinct from each other yet complementary to each other.

There are, then, undoubted similarities between the account of the human person in the person theory and the account of the Person of the divine Son in the Chalcedonian definition. The similarities operate at the most basic level of human thought, where the subject to be grappled with is what it means for something to be. This is what ontology does. The similarities are, we might say, 'structural', in that they describe some very basic features of what it is for an individual to be a human person or a divine Person. I claim there is sufficient in common between the two descriptions to justify further exploration. Already an exciting prospect is beginning to emerge, viz. that of updating the patristic analogy between the divine and human in Christ and the mind and body in the individual, and using a very different and contemporary kind of philosophy in the attempt.

The human person and the divine Person

As a next step I shall take a passage from Strawson which contains the main features of his concept of a person (some of it was quoted in chapter 2) and set it out in parallel with a matching statement about the Person of Christ. This matching statement on the right reproduces the statement on the left except for the following alterations. Where the left-hand column refers to 'persons' or 'person' the right-hand column refers to 'Person of Christ'. Where the left-hand column refers to the derived conscious and corporeal states of the person, the right-hand column refers to 'Godhood' and 'humanhood' or 'divine' and 'human'. I shall then identify four features of the account of the human person on the left and inquire to what extent these features may be attributable to the divine Person on the right and how far the analogical statement about the divine Person is consistent with traditional Christology. At every stage, though, we must keep in mind the two golden rules for treating analogies: they may illustrate but they do not demonstrate; and where there are similarities there are dissimilarities also.

THE HUMAN PERSON	THE DIVINE PERSON
' . . . a necessary condition of states of consciousness being ascribed at all is that they should be ascribed to the	' . . . a necessary condition of GODHOOD being ascribed at all is that it should be ascribed to the *very*

very same thing as certain corporeal characteristics, a certain physical situation, etc. That is to say, states of consciousness could not be ascribed at all, *unless* they were ascribed to persons, in the sense I have claimed for this word. We are tempted to think of a person as a sort of compound of two kinds of subjects: a subject of experiences (a pure consciousness, an ego) on the one hand, and a subject of corporeal attributes on the other. Many questions arise when we think in this way.'[8]

same thing as certain HUMAN characteristics, a certain physical situation, etc. This is to say, GODHOOD could not be ascribed at all, *unless* it was ascribed to the PERSON OF CHRIST, in the sense I have claimed for this word. We are tempted to think of THE PERSON OF CHRIST as a sort of compound of two kinds of subjects: a DIVINE subject on the one hand, and a subject of HUMAN attributes on the other. Many questions arise when we think in this way.'

First, there is a logical priority of the concept of person over the mental and physical states which derive from this priority. Strawson contends that <u>conscious states can only be had by individuals who are also bodies</u>. There is <u>no possibility of a subject of conscious states being immaterial</u>. Conscious states and corporeal characteristics are to be ascribed '*to the very same thing*'. Second, there is an *actual* (not merely logical) unity of the person as the subject, of both physical and mental states. This is the 'sense' which Strawson says he has 'claimed for this word'. 'We are tempted to think of a person as a sort of compound of two kinds of subjects . . . Many questions arise when we think in this way.' The person is the one ontological subject of both kinds of states. Strawson's claim is easily confirmable by the very general experience of being a person, for we are each the sort of individual he has described. We are rarely aware of any division within ourselves of the kind philosophers introduce into their talk about conscious states. We take our individual unity for granted. Thinking about doing something (like having lunch) and doing it are different activities but they are not so different that we need a doctrine of interaction of substances – one mental, one physical – to explain the difference.

Arising from these two features of the concept of the person, i.e. its logical priority over mental and physical states and the real ontological unity of the person which gives rise to them, we may now add a third, namely that the person theory insists that the <u>person is not reducible to either mental or physical states.</u> A person is not to be regarded as a compound of 'pure consciousness' and 'corporeal attributes'; equally banished is the reductive attempt to regard the person as essentially 'a pure consciousness' or only 'a subject of corporeal attributes'. Fourth, we may remark that the person theory provides an effective conceptual veto against at least some of its rival theories. This veto depends on the logical priority of the person. A 'necessary condition' has been built into the concept. If <u>a thing is either a mind or a body, or if a thing turns out to</u>

be two things (a mind and a body), then that thing cannot be a person.

These four features of the person theory are logical rules which govern the use of the concept 'person'. Now let us return to the analogical statement about the Person of Christ in the right-hand column, where we will find these same logical rules deliberately reproduced. Remarkably, all four of the rules do apply to the Person of Christ as that doctrine is set forth in Christian teaching.

First, there is a logical priority of the Person of Christ over the derivatives 'Godhood' and 'humanhood' which are also applicable to him. In more orthodox language, there is priority for the one divine Person over the divine and human natures. Can it be maintained, as my analogy does, that 'a necessary condition of Godhood being ascribed at all is that it should be ascribed to the *very same thing* as certain human characteristics, a certain physical situation, etc.'? At first glance this looks an unacceptably limiting condition to impose on Godhood. Nevertheless this 'necessary condition' expresses in its own way what turns out to be orthodox belief about the incarnation of God in Christ. This is because God, through the Person of Christ, became man and assumed a human nature. It is therefore most appropriate to say, after the incarnation, that Godhood must be ascribed to the same thing as certain human characteristics. We shall return to this important point later in the chapter.

Second, there is an actual ontological unity of the Person who is the one subject of divine and human attributes. As we have seen, this was the main issue at Chalcedon. Talk of God is now grounded in a historical human life, as the parallel statement makes clear. Because of Jesus Christ a rewriting of the rules governing talk of God is necessary which grounds them in the event of the incarnation. Without the anchorage of God-talk in 'certain human characteristics, a certain physical situation, etc.' which are provided by the incarnation, it will remain insufficiently Christocentric and will fail to register that, for Christians, the incarnation is and remains the primary theological datum.

Third, the divine Person cannot be reduced to the two separate natures, and cannot be identified with either. Our analogical statement reads 'We are tempted to think of the Person of Christ as a sort of compound of two kinds of subjects: a divine subject on the one hand, and a subject of human attributes on the other. Many questions arise when we think in this way.' Christian doctrine has in fact always guarded against this temptation. The one Christ is acknowledged in two natures, but reference to either nature is distorted unless it is first understood as applying to the single subject of the divine Son. In Christology the counterpart to Cartesian dualism is Nestorianism, which at any rate according to its critics

was thought to posit two separate natures, to one or the other of
which different predicates might be variously assigned. While such
a position safeguarded the reality of Christ's physical life, its main
difficulty, doubtless exaggerated by its opponents, lay in its separation of the two natures with the result that the relation of each to
the other became problematic and the unity of the one Son became
impaired. The Person cannot be identified with either of the
natures.

Fourth, let us observe that an 'irreducibility requirement' operates on both sides of the analogy. Descriptions of human persons
are not reducible to descriptions of mental or physical states, just as
descriptions of bodily behaviour are not reducible to descriptions
of responses to stimuli. An obvious analogy suggests itself in
Christology. Descriptions of the Person of Christ are not reducible
to descriptions of either his divine nature or his human nature.
Each description isolated from the other distorts the character of
the single ontological subject. We may fairly say that an irreducibility requirement is a robust component of the Chalcedonian
definition and one which finds its way into our parallel.

New logical rules for 'God'

The comparison between the human person and the divine Person
has resulted in logical rules being uncovered which govern each.
The emphasis on the divine unity may be pressed a little further.
We have seen how the person theory grounds separate sets of
predicates in the single ontological subject, the person. Classical *Lutheran*
theologians who wished to speak of the one Christ made known in
two natures used the doctrine of the 'communication of attributes'
(*communicatio idiomatum*). The doctrine states that 'while the human and Divine natures in Christ were separate, the attributes of
one may be predicated of the other in view of their union in the one
Person of the Saviour'.[9] Pope Leo's use of the doctrine, for example, allowed him to say that the Son of Man is read of as descend-
ing from heaven (John 3.13) and the Son of God is said to have
been crucified (1 Corinthians 2.8).[10] This double attribution to the
one divine Person cannot but remind us of the body-and-mind
unity posited by the person theory. In each case, the philosophical
and the christological, the essential feature is the protection of the
unity of the subject.

The person theory exercises a conceptual veto on the extremes
of Cartesian dualism and outright materialism. It does so by insisting on the monistic unity of the person, for once this unity is lost
the way is open to regard the now divided subject as an instance of
one of its parts. The Chalcedonian definition of the Person of
Christ operates a similar kind of conceptual veto against heresy.
Cartesians, we may say, first destroy the unity of the person and

then make persons essentially minds; an ancient christological parallel is provided by the Homoiousians of the fourth century. In conceding that the Son is only *like* the Father, yet not identical with him, the separation between the human historical person of Jesus and the Godhood of God the Father automatically occurs. But some modern theology is in danger of effecting just this separation of the divine and the human, thus breaching what has been called the 'irreducibility requirement' of the catholic faith. Once talk of God is severed from its theological instantiation in Jesus Christ, the way is opened for alternative concepts of God to become established whose relationship to Jesus Christ is, to say the least, problematic. Pantheism, deism, liberalism and idealism all provide examples of a God whose being is severed from the being of Jesus. The widespread idea of an undifferentiated God, equally active in the world's religions, is itself the product of the separation of the idea of God from its concrete embodiment in Jesus Christ. Since Jesus *is* God, commendation of this God apart from Jesus merely underlines the logical mistake that gives rise to it.

The person theory is a product of ontology. It operates at a fundamental level of thinking where basic structural issues are at stake. A confident comparison may be made between the structural issues raised by the human person and those raised by the Person of Christ. Such are the similarities between them that it becomes possible to regard the person theory as a useful diagnostic instrument for drawing attention to the neglect of ontology in current theological debate. One example, already mentioned, is the direction of some liberal theology towards a psilanthropism where Jesus is only and merely a person, or at any rate not God in the full sense intended by the *homoousion* clause of the Chalcedonian definition ('one in being with the Father as touching the Godhead . . . '). A related example concerns the conduct of what is sometimes called the 'inter-religious dialogue'. There could hardly be a more important area for Christians to be engaging in, in an attempt to understand their sisters and brothers in the non-Christian faiths. But this cannot be done by intellectual dilutions of Christian faith the implications of which, when they are recognized and understood by practising Christians, generally scandalize them. In a much-discussed essay John Hick advocated a 'Copernican revolution' in theology which 'involves a shift from the dogma that Christianity is at the centre to the realization that it is *God* who is at the centre, and that all the religions of mankind, including our own, serve and revolve around him'.[11] The God at the centre is 'the God of universal love, the creator and Father of all mankind, [who] wills the ultimate good and salvation of all men'.[12] This Christians do of course believe. The problem, however, is that they also believe *more* than this. The God of universal love is acknowledged by Christians because he became incarnate in Jesus Christ. The removal of this actual, particular revelation of God in a real historical human being is the impossible price which must be paid for installing the universal undifferentiated God at the centre of all the religions without distinction. This is a failure in ontology. That is why the issue has been raised now. The being of God in the second Person of the Trinity united to itself a human nature. (An attempt to translate the doctrine into a more modern idiom will be made in chapter 6.) The incarnation of God the Son is the union of Godhood and humanhood, akin to the logically irreducible subject of the person theory. This union has given Christian theology new logical rules for speaking of God at all. If Christianity is to engage in serious dialogue with non-Christians, and to do so as Christianity, then it cannot sign away its distinctive features in advance and expect to retain any respect. The logical rules anchor talk of God in the historical individual Jesus of Nazareth. They have redirected the channels through which the thinking of Christians about God must flow.

The uniqueness of the Christian doctrine of God in relation to the theism of most of the religions of the world is fully consistent with a positive, open attitude to those religions. Christians have reason to be grateful for the knowledge of God exclusively revealed to them in Jesus Christ; they also have reason to be grateful for what they find of God in the non-Christian religions. The best cure for a narrow exclusivism is simply to meet men and women of other faiths, and to learn from their experience and devotion. Yet often in this book I shall be referring to the doctrines of the incarnation and the Trinity in the belief that they tell us something about what God is and what God has done, and these are unique to Christianity. This position does not make me an 'exclusivist' who believes that only in the Christian faith is there salvation and truth. The approach adopted, if it must be labelled at all, is that of 'inclusivism', which 'affirms the salvific presence of God in non-Christian religions while still maintaining that Christ is the definitive and authoritative revelation of God'.[13] Pluralism, the position 'that other religions are equally salvific paths to the one God',[14] is rejected. One good reason for rejecting pluralism is that those Christians who advocate it usually manage to relativize what are generally taken to be the central claims of Christian faith to such an extent that their position is scarcely consistent with historical Christianity. Of course I beg the question how we tell whether any particular theological position is consistent with historical Christianity. But there must be other ways of entering into dialogue with people from the other faiths without rendering optional, or even unrecognizable, the great truths of the Christian faith.

Getting the method right

A further gain from the comparison between the human 'person' and the divine 'Person' is that it illustrates a principle of procedure which is common to all inquiry, viz. that the method of inquiry must be determined by its object. With regard to inquiry in the sciences, Arthur Peacocke has described how nature confronts science as a 'hierarchy of natural systems'[15] each of which presents the human mind with a different level of complexity. Each level in turn demands an appropriate set of concepts to explicate it. The hierarchy which confronts science has given rise to two opposite dangers. In one, reductionism, higher levels of organization are interpreted by the concepts which belong to lower levels (as when persons are regarded as 'just' bundles of atoms). In the other, vitalism, it is believed 'that some entitites or forces, other than physiochemical ones, are present and operate in biological organisms and constitute their distinctiveness as "living" organisms'.[16] An important feature of the person theory is that it starts in an appropriate place. In ruling out Cartesianism it rules out vitalism, for it refuses to make the desperate appeal to the existence of immaterial substances in order to protect the uniqueness of persons among species. But it also vetoes the reduction of persons to living bodies explicable organically without remainder. The Chalcedonian ground rules for the use of the concept of the Person of Christ are similar. Chalcedon does not suppose a modern view of a natural hierarchy with the divine Son at its apex. But it rules out a vitalism that makes our Lord's divinity some further level of being, conveniently unavailable to observation and historical inquiry; equally (and obviously) it excludes a reductive approach to Christ which assumes that what is to be understood can be sufficiently explicated in human terms. In each case the subject being inquired into is allowed to determine the method of inquiry appropriate to it and the concepts necessary to explicate it. In each case the ontological language forbids the 'reductive slide' from getting started.

There is one more feature of the person theory which invites comparison with a similar theme in Christology. The person theory treats persons as logical subjects which generate double sets of predicates; and they are the only beings to do so. The theory therefore ascribes to persons what might be called 'a guarantee of uniqueness'. Strawson calls these predicates 'M-predicates' and 'P-predicates'. They correspond to the 'corporeal characteristics' and 'states of consciousness' in our earlier parallel. M-predicates, he says, are

> properly applied to material bodies to which we would not dream of applying predicates ascribing consciousness . . . they include things like 'weighs 10 stone', 'is in the drawing-room', and so on. The second kind

consists of all the other predicates we apply to persons . . . They will
include things like 'is smiling', 'is going for a walk', as well as things like
'is in pain', 'is thinking hard', 'believes in God', and so on.[17]

We must not be too troubled by the rather blurred dividing line
between the two sets. Dogs go for walks and experience pain, but
they don't believe in God or do countless other things that persons
do. One can either tighten up the criteria for what is to count as a
P-predicate, or introduce 'a special subclass of predicates within
the class of P-predicates',[18] the defining characteristic of which is
their peculiarity to persons.

Double predication is a fairly common feature of recent
Christology and the next chapter is devoted to it. We have already
seen how Chalcedon adopts double sets of predicates in setting
forth what is to be believed about Jesus Christ. The person theory,
with its M- and P-predicates, provides us with a working model of
double-predication. According to the person theory M-predicates
are shared by persons and non-persons. In the Chalcedonian definition some predicates emphasize the solidarity of the Person of
Christ with human persons. He is 'truly man', 'one in being with us
as touching the manhood', and so on. Other predicates could only
be truly ascribed to one who was also God and have no earthly
parallels. In terms of our comparison these double predicates ascribe Godhood and humanhood to the single Christ as M- and
P-predicates ascribe states of consciousness and corporeal characteristics to the single entity, the person. Strawson's explanation of
these predicates helps to bring out analogically the unique character of what is believed about Jesus. He says we normally 'would not
dream' of applying P-predicates to material bodies, yet in the case
of persons we must. Analogously we would not dream of ascribing
'deity-predicates' to a human being. Yet this is exactly what the
Christian faith does and must continue to do if it is to remain
Christian. To designate an individual as a person is to confer on
him or her a status which only members of that species have. This
is a fact acknowledged by the ascription to persons, and only persons, of P-predicates. To designate Jesus Christ as Son of God is
also to confer on him a unique status among all men and women
whose being he also shares. No other human person is 'only-
begotten God, Word, Lord, Jesus Christ'. Of no one else would
Christians ever say that he or she was 'perfect in Godhead . . .
perfect in humanhood'.

I think the comparison which has been attempted in this chapter
shows an impressive structural similarity between the two concepts
of person. It is impressive because what has been claimed for the
Person of Christ has not been derived from the analogy; rather the
analogy has been used to illustrate what is already essential to the
Christian tradition. The degree of similarity between the human

person and the divine Person helps to establish confidence in the basic analogy and to suggest a promising line of defence of traditional Christology. If there is any warrant for comparing the irreducible unity of body and mind which a person is with the irreducible unity of God and man that the Person of Christ is, then those who would proscribe as unintelligible the basic Christian belief that Jesus Christ is 'truly God and truly man' would do well to ponder whether the person theory provides them with the very model they complain is missing.

What, though, of the *dis*similarities between the human person and the divine Person? The human person is temporal and created; the divine Person 'begotten of the Father before the ages . . .' The human person is a sinner awaiting redemption; the divine Person is the sinless redeemer. These and other dissimilarities must also be emphasized and will be considered in later chapters. None the less a basis for comparison between the human person and the divine Person remains, which, because of the doctrine that God has made us in his image, we might perhaps have dimly expected. Enough has been done at the ontological level to make a case for some structural similarities between the human person and the divine Person which is strong enough to warrant further exploration. So far only a start has been made, and modifications will become necessary as we proceed.

NOTES

1   A. Grillmeier s j, *Christ in Christian Tradition* (London: Mowbray, ²1975), pp. 410–13.
2   *Third Letter to Nestorius*, 4e, 8a–b. Text in, e.g., J. Stevenson (ed.), *Creeds, Councils and Controversies* (London: S P C K, 1972), pp. 282, 284. Emphasis added.
3   Grillmeier, *Christ in Christian Tradition*, part 2, pp. 153–439.
4   ibid., pp. 308–28.
5   ibid., p. 380.
6   Text in, e.g., Stevenson, *Creeds, Councils and Controversies*, p. 337, reproduced here *verbatim*. Elsewhere in this book I have followed John Macquarrie's suggestion that 'of one substance with' (*homoousios*) be translated 'one in being with'.
7   R. V. Sellers, *The Council of Chalcedon* (London: S P C K, 1953), p. 212. Emphasis added.
8   P. F. Strawson, *Individuals* (London: Methuen, 1959), p. 102. In this passage Strawson criticizes both Cartesianism and (p. 95) the 'no ownership' theory of the self. I have excluded this from the discussion.
9   E. A. Livingstone (ed.), *The Concise Oxford Dictionary of the Christian Church* (Oxford: Oxford University Press, 1977), p. 120.
10 *Tome* 5. See Sellers, *The Council of Chalcedon*, p. 240. Pope Leo says Jesus Christ is 'one Person of twofold form' (p. 243).
11 J. Hick, 'The Copernican Revolution in Theology' in *God and the Universe of Faiths* (Glasgow: Collins, 1977), p. 131.
12 ibid., p. 122.

13 Gavin d'Costa, *Theology and Religious Pluralism* (Oxford: Basil Blackwell, 1986), p. 80.
14 ibid., p. 22.
15 Arthur Peacocke, *Creation and the World of Science* (Oxford: Clarendon Press, 1979), p. 113.
16 ibid., p. 118.
17 Strawson, *Individuals*, p. 104.
18 Richard Swinburne, *The Coherence of Theism* (Oxford: Clarendon Press, 1977), p. 101.

CHAPTER 4

One Person – Two Languages

Recently several theologians have drawn on the idea that Jesus Christ is a single individual about whom it becomes necessary to speak in two languages. None of them, however, anchors the determination to speak in this double way about Christ in the more familiar context of speaking about persons, nor do they seem aware of the parallels between the two subjects which we have begun to explore. In this chapter I first describe the use of the two-language motif in some recent Christology and show how its potentiality has yet to be recognized. I then describe the principle of complementarity in order to assess whether the double languages used in Christology are genuinely complementary. I shall agree that, for ontological reasons, complementary languages must be spoken about the human person, and that these reasons apply yet more strongly in the special case of the Person of Christ. However, recent attempts to do this will be criticized, since they fail to distinguish adequately between the different ontological levels involved and they abandon, or appear to ignore, the original ontological reasons for speaking complementary languages at all. They are reductionist. Thomas Morris's recent attempt to defend a strong identity between Jesus and God is then contrasted with them, and a *via media*, based on the analogical approach to the Person of Christ, is preferred to liberal and conservative accounts.

Liberal Christology: two languages

Both sides in the recent discussion over *The Myth of God Incarnate* have used the double-language motif with reference to Christ. So Frances Young admits to finding herself

> driven to tell *two* stories, to think in terms of two models, which cannot be fitted together in a literal way, or spelled out in relation to one another, but which in some sense reflect both the 'scientific' model of the world which my culture forces upon me and the 'mythological' model from which my religious faith cannot escape . . .

One language 'finds explanations of phenomena, behaviour and events in terms of natural causes'; the other refers to realities which are not only inaccessible to the normal methods of scientifc investigation, but are also indefinable in terms of human language, and in their totality, inconceivable within the limited powers and expe-

rience of the finite human mind'.[1] Bishop Christopher Butler in a
spirited defence of the Chalcedonian definition rightly holds

> that we can affirm about this single historical figure [of Jesus] a double
> series of predicates. One series is such as we could predicate of anyone
> else: that he was fully human, a body-and-soul human being, with a
> human mother, 'like us in all things' . . . The other series of predicates
> are such as we can only attribute to God. . . [2]

Edward Schillebeeckx speaks of two 'language-games' which must
be kept apart when explicating the meaning of Christ. There is a
'secular language' and a 'religious language', and they operate at
different 'levels' and both contribute to 'the inevitable "two-
language" evaluation of one and the same reality'.[3] There is a
'duality of total aspects' in Jesus Christ, and medieval as well as
modern versions of the person concept are said to display 'dual
aspects'.[4] But while Schillebeeckx wrestles with the relation between the divine Person of Christ and the human person Jesus, and
commends Strawson and Ryle for what light they have shed on the
concept of a person, it does not occur to him to develop their
solutions in order to help him out of his difficulties with the classical doctrine.

One must turn to the work of Maurice Wiles and John Robinson,
both of whom may have influenced Frances Young, to see a developed use of the double-language motif.[5] In his much-discussed
paper 'Does Christology Rest on a Mistake?' Wiles affirms that
Christians have used two distinct types of language when speaking
of Jesus. They have told different stories, a human historical story
and a divine mythological story. This second story, we are told, has
a different character, a different function and a different logical
behaviour from the first, with the result that the divinity of Christ is
to be understood more as an interpretative category than a factual
reality. Once the logical distinctiveness of each language is understood, much of the confusion which accompanies traditional formulations of the christological problem is thought to be avoided.
The doctrine of the incarnation of God in Christ belongs to the
second story, so that language about the divinity of Christ is one
particular interpretation of his significance rather than a factual
account of his divinity which has its referent in some mysterious
addition to his humanity.[6] Christological statements, then, are
combinations of two stories, one empirical and descriptive, the
other mythological and interpretative. To locate the divinity of
Christ in the second kind of story is not to deny it but to classify it.
In cosmology too, Wiles continues, we tell two stories, one the
scientific story of evolution, the other the 'frankly mythological
story' of the creation and fall, so that 'if we know what we are doing
we can weave the two stories together in poetically creative ways'.

He still wants, in common with all Christians, to see 'the life and death of Jesus as a part of the human story which is of unique significance in relation to seeing the human story as a whole as a true story of divine redemption at work'.[7]

Robinson develops Wiles's thoughts on the two stories further. Christians, he says, talk not about 'two storeys, but two stories. The one is natural, scientific, descriptive. The other is supernatural, mythological and interpretative.' A dualism of languages is allowed to replace a dualism of natures, and talk about the supernatural is no longer to be understood as a 'parallel, superior causal sequence, but an interpretation, a *re-velatio* or turning back of the veil, in terms of myth or a "second" story, of the same process studied by science and history'.[8] For Robinson the doctrine of the sinlessness of Jesus, as well as his uniqueness, perfection and finality, is to be understood as belonging to the second language. That Jesus is sinless expresses a theological judgement rather than a true synthetic proposition extrapolated from the available historical evidence. The judgement, of course, is unlikely to have arisen had there not been sound historical reasons for affirming it. But what is important here is the recognition that 'sinlessness' belongs in an interpretative context in which the death of Jesus is presented as 'the perfect sacrifice for sin'. It is a very important element in the interpretative story, an element which would continue to stand without the historical probability (which would in any case be impossible to substantiate) that Jesus was at all times somehow objectively free from sin. Considerations of this kind are responsible for the title of Robinson's paper, 'Need Jesus Have Been Perfect?' If the view was held, or if it could be shown historically, that the empirical life of Jesus included some 'imperfections', this would not affect the theological doctrine of Christ's perfection, since that doctrine is an interpretation of the life of Jesus, an evaluation, not a straightforward description.

Can complementarity help?

The parallels between two-story Christology and the double-predicate person theory are striking. Peter Baelz rightly calls the former 'the thesis of complementary languages'.[9] Complementarity is widely discussed in science and religion and can be a promising principle of method in certain cases.[10] Because of its use in Christology it is necessary to state very briefly what is meant by it. According to a standard statement of the complementarity principle given by D. M. MacKay, two or more descriptions can qualify as complementary if four conditions can be satisfied. They must each have a common reference. Together, they must be capable of providing, in principle, an exhaustive account of the common reference. Each description must however make a different assertion.

And this is because the logical preconditions for each description must be mutually exclusive.[11] The complementarity principle was designed to reconcile apparently conflicting statements about natural phenomena. It was first promulgated by the distinguished physicist Niels Bohr in order to overcome certain problems in the new field of quantum mechanics, not least the problem of how light can be alternatively conceived of as waves or particles.[12] Bohr himself later came to hold the view that the wave-particle duality was to be resolved not by invoking the complementarity principle but by examining 'the experimental conditions under which the complementary phenomena appear'.[13]

A recent summary of the debate about wave-particle duality states that 'all forms of energy-carrying radiation exhibit both wave and particle aspects, whether it be electromagnetic radiation, such as light and X-rays, or beams of electrons, protons, atoms, molecules, or large objects such as stones and billiard-balls'. 'The language of waves' is used in describing 'how the radiation moves from one location to another'; but 'the language of particles' is used in describing 'how the radiation is emitted and how it behaves when it reaches its destination and interacts with matter'.[14] Clearly, then, the ontological pattern is familiar. A single phenomenon is thought to give rise to two 'aspects', and the aspects give rise to different 'languages', each of which do different jobs. Theologians may be interested to learn that physicists are not through yet with complementarity. As we shall see, a useful refinement of complementarity is the hierarchical version where apparently conflicting statements can be complementary because they operate on different logical levels. As examples of different levels MacKay cites '(1) a mathematician's and an engineer's descriptions of what is going on in a computer . . . (2) mentalistic and physicalistic descriptions of a person's behaviour, (3) theological and scientific accounts of the same situation or event'.[15] The assumption that reality consists of several levels of being, 'nature's hierarchies',[16] each of which is studied by the appropriate science, is commonly supposed, though the metaphor 'levels' must not preclude overlaps between them.[17] Indeed a 'Christology of levels' may be said to be embedded in the New Testament. Using what appears to be a fixed formula[18] St Paul speaks of God's Son, 'Jesus Christ our Lord, which was made of the seed of David according to the flesh; and declared to be the Son of God with power, according to the spirit of holiness . . .' (Romans 1.3–4, AV). The passage contains what may fairly be called 'complementary descriptions' which give two different estimations of their common reference. The New English Bible purposefully adopts the 'levels' metaphor in translating 'according to' (*kata*): '. . . on the human level he was born of David's stock, but on the level of the spirit – the Holy Spirit – he was declared Son of God by a mighty act in that he rose from the dead'.

I think double-language Christology does provide a genuine case of complementarity. Each language has a common reference. Both are needed for the whole truth to be told. Genuinely different assertions are offered by each. And the logical preconditions for language about God and language about a person are, at least in important respects, 'mutually exclusive'. Unfortunately, so far little has been achieved merely by identifying and speaking complementary languages about Jesus Christ. There are two main reasons for this. First, taking our cue from what has been observed in the previous paragraph about levels, the different ontological levels on which the separate languages operate have been ignored. In the summary quoted earlier physicists speak of 'the language of waves' and 'the language of particles'. This distinction is made at the cost of making the term 'language' imprecise, for wave-talk and particle-talk belong easily to the single language of physics and operate on the same scientific 'level'. Yet when Jesus Christ is confessed both as a Person of God and as a human being two levels are clearly brought together which are ontologically and qualitatively different. Jesus Christ is 'the light of the world' (John 8.12). Is the light which Jesus is to be understood as wave-like or corpuscular? The very foolishness of the question is the measure of the difference between the two christological stories and the ontological levels they presuppose.

This difficulty over different levels need not be fatal. It is possible to invoke the alternative hierarchical version of the complementarity thesis in such a way that due regard is given to the differences between them. But the second difficulty cannot be resolved so easily. Double-language Christology has developed as a matter of convenient methodology, and not as a matter of ontology. The charge of neglect of basic issues of ontology was laid against Hick's Copernican revolution in theology in the last chapter and it is being repeated now. In physics the complementarity principle was a device for reconciling apparently diverse approaches to the phenomenon of light. Elsewhere it is used for holding together science and theology as complementary perspectives on reality, and in discussions of the free will problem the principle is sometimes thought to make possible complementary explanations of human actions. However, with regard to the Person of Christ we may safely say it is the unique, logically irreducible, subject of his Person, consubstantial with the Father, consubstantial with us, which makes the use of complementary languages unavoidable. What Jesus Christ is in being both divine and human is what makes necessary the ascription of double predicates. Using both languages, then, is the least inadequate way of telling the whole truth about him. Ontology precedes methodology, as being precedes describing. Simply by being the divine Person he is, complementary stories, divine and human, must be told.

The alternative, analogical approach

Let us suppose now that a precedent were sought which would help to amplify the claim that there are ontological subjects which, just by being the subjects they are, generate double languages. We have one, of course, in the human person. Persons *do* provide an actual case where double aspects inescapably arise, and these are what generate logically distinct, yet complementary, descriptions. There is an ontological warrant for them in the unique, irreducible subjects they are which is confirmed in the actual experience of being a person. Our analogy developed in the last chapter lies at hand for building similarities between the unitary being of a person and the unitary being of the Christ who is made known in two natures. How an individual is both fully God and fully human is a mystery, as the Church has always maintained (chapter 8). Those who would claim that the mystery is a theological liability, an obstacle to faith and not the object of faith, might well wish to reconsider the mystery which each of us is in simply being a person. Indeed, being a person is the very general experience which helps us compare the unfamiliar (the Person of Christ) with the familiar (ourselves), for as we have seen, the need to speak of persons by means of complementary series of predicates arises from the need to demonstrate the unity of the person against dualism and to guard against reduction. The Chalcedonian definition has parallel theological aims. With its emphasis on a single subject made known in two natures, it might itself be designated a fine example of complementarity, long before that ugly modern word was coined.

In particle physics two types of explanation of the behaviour of light operate at the same level. According to the person theory M- and P-predicates operate at different levels while the ontological subject is the one subject of both. With the divine Person of Christ the distinction between the levels is vast, since one of them is divine, the other human. But the one subject again embraces both, despite the distinctions between them, and our understanding of this subject's unity-in-duality is aided by the convenient analogy with the human person. The appropriateness of this analogy may now be taken a step further. The Chalcedonian definition stipulates that the one Christ is 'to be acknowledged in two natures, without confusion, without change, without division, without separation'. These four adverbs can be readily applied to the ontology of a human person (which is not to say the Chalcedonian fathers had any such comparison in mind). Indeed it will deepen the analogy between the human person and the divine Person to make the application, and may give us guidance from the past about how to handle modern discussions about ontological levels.

Let us take the M- and P-predicates which apply to the human person in the person theory and ask whether it is intelligible to say of these predicates, and the aspects of the person they refer to, that they coexist 'without confusion, without change, without division, without separation'. The answer is clearly affirmative. We have already seen that a thought (ascribed by a P-predicate) can never be 'confused' with a brain process (ascribed by a M-predicate).[19] Mature personhood cannot be 'changed' into the sort of reality that M-predicates could explicate. The experienced unity of being a person remains 'without division' by the distinction between M- and P-predicates, and also 'without separation', since any suggestion of the independent sufficiency of either realm would lead to dualism and its attendant problems and break the irreducibility requirement. The analogy here between human persons and the Person of Christ may be extended even to the further qualifying phrases 'the distinction of natures being in no way abolished because of the union, but rather the characteristic property of each nature being preserved, and concurring into one Person and one subsistence'. The stipulations made here accord fully with the logical rules governing the concepts 'person' and 'Person' which were set out in the last chapter.

The person analogy has been used to illustrate what the Church teaches about Jesus already. By illustrating some of the ontological issues at stake it shows that the reasons for talking in complementary languages about the human person and about the divine Person of Christ are grounded in ontology. The analogy enables us to diagnose why the stimulating attempt to apply the complementary language thesis to Christology finally falters, because in the end it is not grounded in the full reality of Christ's person. If Christ is not really and fully divine, the grounds for ascribing deity to him at all in one of the two complementary languages the Church speaks about him are worryingly absent. Wiles's approach to the Person of Christ evacuates the ontological content. What he leaves himself with is still capable of having the complementary languages label appended to it, but the reasons for talking the two languages have disappeared. Unless Jesus is God in his very being, why play the language-game of deity? Wiles says that 'the heart of the suggestion' he wants to make is that traditional Christology rests on the mistake of supposing 'that the full divine character of redemption in Christ could only be maintained if the person and act of the redeemer were understood to be divine in a direct and special sense'. The doctrines of incarnation and redemption will require us to tell two stories, 'But we do not need – indeed on this analysis we would be wrong – to tie the two stories together by claiming that at one particular point, namely the life, death and resurrection of Jesus of Nazareth, the two stories are literally united with one another.'[20] An alternative view is that the incarnate Christ presents his Church with an obligation to tell two stories about him, stories which do not need to be 'tied together' because in the Gospels and the Church's faith they have not come apart.

In support of this view we now have a developing analogy which enables us to illustrate something of how a historical individual could be 'truly God and truly man': the analogy is with how a person is the same subject of M- and P-predicates. Christian faith reconstructs talk of God by anchoring it in the historical and ontological reality of Jesus. After Jesus the logic of 'God' has new rules. Versions of Christology which hold that the divinity of Jesus is a mistake or that the incarnation is a myth avoid ontology. They are not determined by the unity of the divine and the human in the one Christ. The great ontological *sine qua non* of the Christian faith, the *homoousion*, is given away. The unity of subject which the analogy with the human person illustrates is not even asserted at all in Wiles's discussion of the incarnation of God in Christ; for him 'we do not need . . . to tie the two stories together'. A notion of God other than that which is embodied in Jesus is brought alongside Jesus and allowed to generate discussion about how each can be woven together. So it becomes a matter of no consequence whether the two stories are formally complementary or not. The ontology giving rise to the two stories has been abandoned. And this ontology is essential to the faith of the Church. The Church has always taught that it is through Christ that we know God in the first place, and ontology tells us why. A doctrine of God which needs subsequently to be tied to Jesus cannot be what Christians understand by 'God'.

The work we have done so far on the person theory and the double predicates it requires enables us to contribute to contemporary discussion about the identity between Jesus and God. A strong statement of incarnational belief, framed (by Maurice Wiles) for its traditional and non-reductive character is 'that Jesus of Nazareth is unique in the precise sense that, while being fully man, it is true of him, and of him alone, that he is also fully God, the Second Person of the co-equal Trinity'.[21] Put this way the doctrine underlines the dilemma facing modern interpreters. On the one hand it successfully rules out that Jesus i) is only a man, ii) is a man who is only like God, iii) is only a man sent by and/or exalted by God, iv) is a man worshipped as God, and v) is God only appearing to be a man. It enables the Church consistently to deny these variants of the faith and to affirm that Jesus Christ is really and completely human, and really and completely divine. On the other hand, however, incarnational faith assumes an identity between Jesus and

God which is clearly vulnerable to simple logical criticism. The suggestion to be made is that the concept of person as it is presented here provides a model of identity which eases the dilemma considerably without impaling its users on the horns of either incoherence or reduction.

A consideration of some of the logical difficulties will show how acute the theological dilemma is.[22] First, in standard examples of identity statements, subject and predicate are reversible. 'Rhodesia is Zimbabwe' and 'the morning star is the evening star' are identity statements where the subject and the predicate are reversible without loss of meaning. Reversibility cannot happen with 'Jesus is God'. If Jesus is God (leaving aside for the moment that Jesus is also 'fully man'), then according to the reversibility rule 'God is Jesus'. But there is more to God than Jesus. Therefore God is not identical with Jesus. Any attempt to press the identity is likely to emulate the 'Christomonism' of some of the 'death of God' theology of the 1960s. A second feature of identity statements is that the copula 'is' means 'is the same as'. The morning star is the same as the evening star. But Jesus is clearly not the same as God. God is three Persons, the Son only one; God creates the world through the Word or Son; the Son is 'sent', the Father is the sender. A third feature of identity statements was used in chapter 2 to expose the shortcomings of the mind/brain identity theory in the philosophy of mind. Objects and events must already belong to the same class, type, etc. before identity claims can be advanced. Because neural events and conscious events belong to different classes, it was suggested, they cannot be identical. Because Jesus is a human being he cannot possibly be God as well. Gods and people are items in different classes.

Conservative Christology: strict identity

We have seen that according to one liberal understanding of the incarnation already discussed in this chapter beliefs about the divinity of Jesus are mythological and interpretatitive, so any claims about Jesus being really God have simply been abandoned. But a strong case for strict and real identity between Jesus and God has recently been made by Thomas V. Morris, whose rigorous work *The Logic of God Incarnate* deserves at least as much theological attention as the mythographers have received. Morris defends the absolute identity between Jesus and God in the more precise form 'Jesus is God the Son'.[23] He accepts a strict principle governing identity statements, the 'indiscernibility of identicals', which amounts to the stipulation that 'a necessary condition for identity is complete commonality of properties'.[24] Any compromise moves, such as the one I am proposing, which is based on the identity of being a single subject of double attributes, automatically fail to satisfy the principle.

In order to make 'Jesus is God the Son' pass the stringent test set by the indiscernibility of identicals, Morris makes some novel moves. The humanity and divinity of Jesus are, he says, 'natural kinds', and 'every such kind has an essence, a set of properties or underlying traits individually necessary and jointly sufficient for membership in the kind'. 'Human nature', then, 'comprises all those properties individually necessary and jointly sufficient for being human'. And any individual who has a divine nature must possess all those properties which belong to the kind-essence of divinity. These include 'omnipotence, omniscience, aseity, eternality, and the like'.[25] And these were had by Jesus in his divine nature, before, during and after his incarnate human life.

An obvious problem with the strong identity thesis between Jesus and God is that there are some human properties like being created, being mortal, being contingent, being ignorant and being able to sin which are incompatible with the same subject also being the bearer of divine properties like being eternal, necessary, omniscient, etc. But here Morris's solution is ingenious. With regard to human properties a further 'crucial distinction' is made between those which are 'common' (but not essential) for being human, like 'living at some time on the surface of the earth',[26] and those which are 'essential' for being human. What counts as an essential property, or what it means for an individual to be essentially human, is shaped by the requirements of the doctrine of the incarnation. A second 'crucial distinction' is made between being 'fully human' and being 'merely human'. 'An individual is fully human just in case he fully exemplifies human nature.'[27] To be 'merely human' is to have 'limitation properties' like being contingent, created, etc.

Armed with these 'metaphysical distinctions' Morris is in a position to defend strict identity between Jesus and God (the Son). Jesus 'was fully human without being merely human'.[28] All properties of his humanity possibly incompatible with his divinity are assigned to 'mere humanity' which, of course, he did not possess. Included among the properties of mere humanity is that of being born! Because Jesus was not merely human he had no need of human paternity.[29] Morris denies that 'type of origin is a kind-essential property for any natural kinds'.[30] 'A philosophical anthropology developed from a distinctively Christian point of view will categorize all human properties logically incompatible with a divine incarnation as, at most, essential to being *merely human.*'[31]

Morris's view of Christ's full humanity, of his two natures, and the 'two minds' view of Christ which he adopts, are all discussed later. Let us concentrate at present on the distinction between full humanity and mere or partial humanity. According to this distinction I have many common properties along with other human

beings, and some essential ones, like those of 'having a body at
some past or present time' and 'having . . . a certain sort of consciousness, a certain sort of experiential field and mental structure'.[32] Indeed these two very general properties may be the only
essential ones. Being fully human means exemplifying fully the
kind-essence of human nature. But this kind-essence is determined
by Morris's own view of what the doctrine of the incarnation allegedly requires. It excludes all that is merely human. Our mortality, contingency and propensity to sin do not belong to 'full
humanity', only to mere humanity, so that Jesus, who was fully
human and not merely human, did not possess them.

I think the distinction between full humanity and mere humanity,
as Morris develops it, is untenable. Morris has provided himself
with a technique whereby any human property allegedly incompatible with the kind-essence of deity is allowed to be relegated from
the class of fully human properties to a new class, the class of
merely human properties. The clear consequence is that in affirming the real humanity of Jesus, what is being affirmed is his complete exemplification of essential, as opposed to common,
humanhood. But it is hard to see, on this view, how the exemplification of a human essence is what Christians affirm when
they affirm Jesus' real humanity. Jesus, in being 'fully human', will
have many common properties of humanity which are essential to
being merely human, but these he will have only contingently. It is
also hard to see how this position is reconcilable with the Chalcedonian statement that Jesus is 'of one substance with us as
touching the manhood, like us in all things apart from sin'. The
classical contrast between our Lord's sinless humanity and our
own sinful humanity is incompatible with Morris's distinction between our Lord's real humanity and our mere humanity. This is
because there are many other properties which our Lord shared
with us, like his contingency, mortality, ignorance, vulnerability,
etc., and his humanity differs from ours in that he had the property
of being able not to sin. Morris's Jesus is in the end scarcely a
human figure at all. His real humanity provides no sort of solidarity
with men and women. It is the exemplification of a human kind-
essence from which many common human properties are excluded. The strong identity between Jesus and God the Son is
preserved and successfully defended. But the price to pay is that of
making Jesus remote from the rest of us who are merely human, a
remoteness which is increased by the doctrine of his two minds
within a single Person (which is criticized in chapter 8).

The 'personal' approach to Christology: a genuine middle way

It is clear that liberal Christology, in emphasizing Jesus' humanity,
has withdrawn from making any identity claims between Jesus and

God the Son. But the conservative reaction, in rightly defending Jesus' real divinity, results in a weak humanity which loses its solidarity with the rest of humankind. It is this impasse which makes the analogical approach to Christology attractive, for it seems to provide, in what we already are as persons, the experience of being a unity embracing fundamentally different characteristics, and this unity provides a fine model for understanding the unity between Jesus and God the Son. There is still further work to be done on the model, but already its usefulness within the discussion of the identity between Jesus and God may now be noted.

Let us make a distinction within the class of identity statements between identity of reference and identity of meaning. This distinction goes back to Aristotle.[33] It is readily applicable to our earlier example 'Rhodesia is Zimbabwe', for while 'Rhodesia' and 'Zimbabwe' are different names referring to the same country, the meanings of the names are different. So even with some straightforward identity statements reference and meaning have to be kept distinct. Now let us consider the innocent statement 'Mary is top of the class'. Both the name 'Mary' and the expression 'top of the class' refer to the same person. There is an identity of reference. Mary is the same person as the person who is top of the class. On the other hand the expression 'top of the class' has a meaning independent of Mary and is of course applicable to other pupils than Mary in other classes. That is because 'is top of the class' is also a simple predicate, and it is not a name as 'Mary' is. The value of the distinction between identity of reference and identity of meaning for Christology should by now be coming into view. Incarnational faith proclaims an identity of reference between Jesus and God. Morris is right to insist that the identity of Jesus is with God the Son, not simply with God. On the one hand 'Jesus' and 'God the Son' refer to the same historical subject, and God the Son really is Jesus. On the other hand 'God the Son' has meanings independent of Jesus which allow us to speak of him as pre-existent, the Word, the second Person of the Trinity. The identity of reference protects a firmly Christocentric theology from reduction, while some difference in meaning between 'Jesus' and 'God' excludes the Christomonism which says 'God is Jesus' without remainder.

The experience of being a (human) person is a fine example of a case where parallel statements or predicates share an identity of reference while retaining a genuine difference of meaning. Wiles's formulation of incarnational orthodoxy (that 'Jesus of Nazareth is unique in the precise sense that, while being fully man, it is true of him, and of him alone, that he is also fully God, the Second Person of the co-equal Trinity') may be interpreted in accordance with it. 'Jesus of Nazareth' is the same as 'God, the Second Person of the

co-equal Trinity'. An ' "is" of identity' is asserted. The same subject is both 'fully man' and 'fully God'. 'Jesus' and the 'Second
Person of the Trinity' have an identity of reference while also differing in meaning. This is because, like M- and P-predicates in the
human case, they operate on different levels and do different jobs,
all the while referring to a single subject. Morris would of course
reject any such account of identity, because it could not pass the
'indiscernibility of identicals' test. Now that identity of meaning
has been separated from identity of reference, it is no longer necessary to insist that subject and predicate should always be reversible.
The third difficulty, that gods and people belong to different
classes, need not bother us either, for, as we saw in chapter 3,
incarnational faith may cause us to alter our categories, and there
remains no good reason for sticking to an inadequate categorical
scheme.

By way of a postscript to the identity issue we may note Nicholas
Lash's helpful suggestion that in classical Christology 'the language
of "person" and "nature" ' . . . was invoked partly in order to help
Christian theology to negotiate the rapids between (straightforward) "identity" and (mere) "predication" '.[34] The person theory
also helps Christian theology to do this. While it offers only analogical help, its illustrative power should not be underestimated. It is
even possible that, in loosening up what can count as an identity
statement, 'identity' is freed from its predominantly mathematical
origins, so that it becomes generally more serviceable, even if the
price to pay is less precision. In this respect 'identity' is like the
concept of equality. Freed from its narrow mathematical application, it has many fruitful uses in moral philosophy.

Double languages, then, must be spoken about Jesus. These
languages arise, not because they provide a convenient methodology with some respectable modern precedents, but because the
being of God-in-Christ demands it. An illustrative analogy was
found in the being of persons. The ontological base uncovered
there is clearly of relevance in two other areas of contemporary
theological debate. First, in the argument whether 'Christology
from below' can be an adequate approach to the Person of Christ[35]
our argument so far suggests that approaches 'from above' and
'from below' are equally necessary. Second, David Brown has recently contributed to the discussion about God in philosophical
theology the important distinction between modern 'theism' and
modern 'deism', characterizing the former as 'interventionist' and
the latter as 'non-interventionist'.[36] This discussion is likely to
continue for several years, and it touches on our theme since in his
analysis of 'deism' Brown singles out, among others, the work of
John Robinson, John Hick and Maurice Wiles, and in some respects his criticisms of them parallel my own. My argument in the

present chapter leads me towards (in Brown's terms) 'interventionism' (though I remain nervous about other claims for this position which Brown makes, especially about how in language God's actions are to be distinguished from our own). Over the next two chapters an alternative approach suggests itself, viz. that language drawn from personal action can do analogical duty for the actions or interventions of God.

NOTES

1   In John Hick (ed.), *The Myth of God Incarnate* (London: S C M Press, 1977), p. 37, also p. 34.

2   In M. Green (ed.), *The Truth of God Incarnate* (London: Hodder & Stoughton, 1977), p. 98.

3   Edward Schillebeeckx, *Jesus* (London: Collins Fount, 1983, 1st pub. 1974), p. 656.

4   ibid., pp. 660, 663.

5   Maurice Wiles, 'Does Christology Rest on a Mistake?' and John Robinson, 'Need Jesus Have Been Perfect?' in S. W. Sykes and J. P. Clayton (eds), *Christ, Faith and History* (Cambridge: Cambridge University Press, 1972), pp. 3–12 and pp. 39–52 respectively.

6   I have outlined Wiles's argument at greater length in my 'Some Recent Developments in Christology', *Baptist Quarterly*, xxvi no. 8 (1976), pp. 335-7.

7   Wiles, 'Does Christology Rest on a Mistake?', p. 11.

8   Robinson, 'Need Jesus Have Been Perfect?', p. 40. See also his *The Human Face of God* (London: S C M Press, 1973), pp. 116–7. Part of Robinson's article reappears here.

9   Peter Baelz, 'A Deliberate Mistake?' in Sykes and Clayton (eds), *Christ, Faith and History*, p. 28.

10 See I. G. Barbour, *Issues in Science and Religion* (London: S C M Press, 1966), pp. 290–4.

11 See D. M. MacKay, 'Complementarity II', *Proceedings of the Aristotelian Society*, supp. vol. xxxii (1958): cit. W. H. Austin, *The Relevance of Natural Science to Theology* (London and Basingstoke: Macmillan, 1976), p. 74.

12 Niels Bohr, 'The Quantum Postulate and the Recent Development of Atomic Theory', *Nature*, cxxi (1928), pp. 580–90.

13 H. A. Bedau, 'Complementarity and the Relation between Science and Religion', *Zygon*, ix (1974), pp. 207–8.

14 Russell Stannard and Noel G. Coley, *Modern Physics and the Problems of Knowledge* (Milton Keynes: Open University Press, 1981), p. 84.

15 D. M. MacKay, ' "Complementarity" in Scientific and Theological Thinking', *Zygon*, ix (1974), pp. 229f.

16 The term 'nature's hierarchies' is found in Arthur Peacocke, *Creation and the World of Science* (Oxford: Clarendon Press, 1979), as the title of section 4 (p. 112).

17 For this and other misconceptions generated by talk of 'levels of being', see the criticism made by Paul Tillich, *Systematic Theology*, Vol. 3 (Digswell Place: Nisbet, 1964), pp. 13–15. He preferred a different metaphor, that of 'dimensions'.

18 See W. Pannenberg, *Jesus – God and Man* (London: S C M Press, 1968), p. 283.

19 Above p. 16.

20 Wiles, 'Does Christology Rest on a Mistake?', pp. 8 and 9.

21 Maurice Wiles, in Hick (ed.), *The Myth of God Incarnate*, p. 1.

22 The logic of identity statements now has an impressive literature. See particularly, Thomas V. Morris, *Understanding Identity Statements* (Aberdeen: Aberdeen University Press, 1984).

23 Thomas V. Morris, *The Logic of God Incarnate* (Ithaca and London: Cornell University Press, 1986), p. 21.

24 ibid. p. 17.

25 ibid., p. 22 and 23.

26 ibid., p. 63.

27 ibid., p. 66.

28 ibid., p. 66.

29 ibid., p. 69.

30 ibid., p. 69.

31 ibid., p. 65 (his emphasis).

32 ibid., p. 145

33 Aristotle *Physics* 1. I am indebted to J. L. Ackrill for his discussion of it in his *Aristotle the Philosopher* (Oxford: Oxford University Press, 1981), p. 26.

34 In Michael Goulder (ed.), *Incarnation and Myth: The Debate Continued* (London: SCM Press, 1979), p. 41.

35 See Colin Gunton, *Yesterday and Today* (London: Darton, Longman & Todd, 1983), chs 2 and 3.

36 David Brown, *The Divine Trinity* (London: Duckworth, 1985), ch. 1.

CHAPTER 5

Person Language and the Person of Christ

In this chapter I suggest that the charge against orthodox Christians of category confusion is itself confused. Arising from the consideration of what a 'category mistake' is a more important suggestion commends itself. It is that the language of Christology which ascribes Godhood to Jesus is importantly similar to the language that the term 'P-predicate' picks out. Then drawing from recent philosophy I identify three features of P-predicates, or 'person language'. These are that it is grounded in the ontology of the person, that it genuinely though indirectly refers, and that it interprets the states of persons, both to themselves and to others. Christological language is then found to have similar features which are identified and developed. If the comparison between the two languages is allowed to stand it may be possible to show that there are important advantages in resisting a tendency to treat christological language as mythological or poetic and in modelling it on person language instead. Finally, the use of the idea of the Word in ancient Christology is found to possess the three features of christological language identified earlier. It will be suggested that the Word, personified in the Old Testament, is now personalized in Jesus, thus confirming the change in the logical rules governing talk of God that the incarnation has brought about. More theological gains from the basic analogy will continue to build up.

Category mistakes in Christology

A further link between the ontology of the human person and the ontology of the incarnation is provided by looking at the use of the term 'category mistake', which plays a crucial role in critical analyses of each. Wiles holds, as the title of his essay 'Does Christology Rest on a Mistake?' suggests, that orthodox Christians have made a mistake. If we ask what kind of mistake, the technical answer is a 'category mistake'.[1] Christians confused their categories in thinking of Jesus as God and as a human being. Happily, the notion of a category mistake is the clue to uncovering the logic of the second language which Christians use about Jesus, not simply because it is a useful analytical tool but because it belongs originally to a rigorous discussion of Cartesian dualism where the ontological status of a human person is at issue. The 'home-field' for the notion of category mistakes is the conquest of mind/body dualism.

Gilbert Ryle introduces the notion in his famous polemic against the dualism of Descartes. He provides a series of well-known illustrations, the first of which is that of the foreigner visiting Oxford.

> A foreigner visiting Oxford or Cambridge for the first time is shown a number of colleges, libraries, playing fields, museums, scientific departments and administrative offices. He then asks 'But where is the University?' . . . It then has to be explained to him that the University is not another collateral institution, some ulterior counterpart to the colleges, laboratories and offices which he has seen. The University is just the way in which all that he has already seen is organized. When they are seen and when their coordination is understood, the University has been seen.[2]

The foreigner's mistake lay, of course, in supposing that 'University' and 'college' were terms in the same category. The particular category mistake which Ryle wanted to expose is the 'official doctrine' which 'represents the facts of mental life as if they belonged to one logical type or category . . . when they actually belong to another. The dogma is therefore a philosopher's myth.'[3] A definition of myth is offered which binds it conceptually to the notion of a category mistake. A myth, writes Ryle, 'is, of course, not a fairy story. It is the presentation of facts belonging to one category in the idioms appropriate to another. To explode a myth is accordingly not to deny the facts but to re-allocate them. And this is what I am trying to do.'[4] Ryle's understanding of what philosophy is follows from the myth-exploding job it does. 'Philosophy is the replacement of category-habits by category-disciplines.'

Wiles and Ryle have parallel targets for criticism, and they share the same conceptual weapons. The parallel is interesting to pursue. Wiles too has an 'official doctrine', the doctrine of the incarnation. He too relies heavily on the notion of a category mistake, and he introduces the term 'myth' into theology with reference to allegedly undetected category mistakes in doctrine. Christians, he says, must not 'succumb to the *category mistake* of confusing the human historical story with the divine *mythological* story'.[5] Both Ryle and Wiles in their different areas assume the great majority of people to be wrong in their basic assumptions. 'Most philosophers, psychologists and religious teachers', admits Ryle, 'subscribe' to the official doctrine of dualism, as even he had once done.[6] Most Christians, thinks Wiles, are wrong in subscribing to the official doctrine of the incarnation, for 'if I am right, the whole of the classical christology would have to be dismissed as resting on a mistake'.[7] Both writers see the exposure of myth as a major concern. Dualism, says Ryle, is 'a philosopher's myth' which must be exploded. It takes little imagination to see that the theologian's myth is the doctrine of the incarnation.

Wiles's essay title 'Does Christology Rest on a Mistake?' obviously bears comparison with H. A. Prichard's 'Does Moral Philosophy Rest on a Mistake?', first published in *Mind* in 1912.[8] The subject-matter bears comparison too, for while Prichard thought it was a mistake to appeal to reason in support of moral obligation Wiles thinks it is a mistake to appeal to divinity 'in a direct and special sense' in support of the doctrine of the incarnation. But, focusing instead upon the central notion of a category mistake, I shall pursue the comparison with Ryle. I think Ryle is right and Wiles is wrong. Ryle is right to attack Cartesian dualism, and the notion of a 'category mistake' is an effective weapon. But Wiles does not take seriously enough that God-in-Christ presents us with an upheaval in our categories so that after the incarnation at least one new category is needed. When the person theory is brought alongside the unrepeatable event of the incarnation, a model is provided which depicts the logical and ontological priority appropriate to the Person of Christ and which also prepares us for the tricky problems of predication which are likely to follow.

The basic issue for Christology is whether the Person of Christ who is truly man and truly God is the primary datum of Christian theology or not. Again, the contrast between 'inclusive' and 'exclusive' is helpful here, for Christians acknowledge that God has been disclosed and continues to be disclosed outside the Christian revelation. They also acknowledge that God is unrepeatably disclosed through the incarnate Son. The requirement must be both to acknowledge the breadth and depth of God's self-revelation in the non-Christian religions while acknowledging also that the revelation through the Son is, for Christians, the decisive unrepeatable expression of God's self-giving. This requirement entails that the particular details of God's self-revelation as Christians understand it are not lost or weakened, but held in open tension with what Christians learn of the Father of Jesus by other names and in other places. If the incarnation is understood primarily as a myth, then one of the obstacles which will be put in the way of a more realistic interpetation of it will be that to bring two different categories together (divinity and humanity) is formally a category mistake. On the other hand, if the incarnation is a primary datum of Christian theology and Jesus is believed to have disclosed what is now to be understood by 'God' there need be no category confusion in bringing them together. In Jesus Christ a new category has appeared, viz. God incarnate, and other categories may have to be rearranged to take into account what has unrepeatably occurred through Jesus Christ. I agree with Morris's contention that it is reasonable for the Christian theologian to allow his or her categories to be shaped by the incarnation.[9] The suggestion that belief in the divinity of Jesus

Christ rests on a category mistake can only be made on the basis of a notion of divinity which Jesus Christ makes redundant.

Some basic features of person language

Let us return to the analogy. Ryle's approach to the mental life of persons is a welcome alternative to dualism and will bring gains to Christology when the language of the latter is compared with the language which we all use in speaking of ourselves, our thoughts, feelings, wishes, etc. Ryle has often been accused of reductionism and behaviourism because he is assumed to have discounted altogether the facts of a person's intellectual, emotional and aesthetic experience. This charge is unfair, but it was anticipated. Ryle wrote:

> In attempting to explode the myth [of dualism] I shall probably be taken to be denying well-known facts about the mental life of human beings, and my pleas that I aim at doing nothing more than rectify the logic of mental conduct concepts will probably be disallowed as mere subterfuge.[10]

All I want to suggest at present is that the character of the language that ascribes Godhood to Jesus is importantly similar to the language which is ascribed to persons and expresses personal states like having intentions or reasons, holding beliefs, reporting feelings, etc. Much of this language consists of the employment of what Ryle called 'mental-conduct words' which dualists misunderstand when they apply them to an independent mental substance. For the moment, though, I shall retain the term 'P-predicate'. I shall draw attention to three general features of P-predicates, and then inquire whether these features can be found already in the language of Christology. If so, we may be able to arrive at some insights into the way the language of Christology works.

First, by definition a P-predicate is ascribable only to a person or persons. This is not merely a remark about language; it is an ontological remark about the kind of being a person is, for the ascription of P-predicates assumes an actual being which gives rise to the need to ascribe certain states to it and to nothing else. The being giving rise to P-predicates is one which has a developed facility for, e.g., communication through language, a developing self-consciousness and a moral awareness; it is one which makes free choices; which is creative (through art and work); which makes relationships, and so on. P-predicates constitute a class of statements which assume that persons have more developed potentialities and qualities than non-persons in the hierarchy of being.

Second, those P-predicates which pick out the mental or emotional states of persons are indirectly referential. Since I shall put considerable weight on this feature of P-predicates I shall describe it at some length, borrowing from Ryle and Wittgenstein in order to supplement what has already been learned from Strawson. Once again the theological gains must await the philosophical exposition. By claiming that P-predicates indirectly refer I mean that i) they do have a referent; but ii) the reference-relation is odd, because iii) the referent is no thing, but a person. The category mistake which Ryle accuses dualists of making is that of treating minds as substantial entities, when they are no such things – indeed that they are _not things_ is precisely the point. The foreigner was mistaken not in thinking there was a University to see, but 'in allocating the University to the same category as that to which the other institutions belong'.[11] Popular vernacular phrases confirm what Ryle contends. People say, 'She has a good mind', 'It was never in my mind', 'Mind that child', 'He is dirty-minded', 'I've got a lot on my mind', and so on. They talk of people being good at mental arithmetic, of being absent-minded, mentally handicapped, and so on. In these and countless other cases 'mind' and 'mental' are words which may optionally be used when, to continue the examples, people want to say someone is clever, innocent, needs to be careful, likes sexual jokes, is worried, is good at doing sums, sometimes acts thoughtlessly, or is someone whose abilities are impaired in some way. None of these colloquial remarks about minds requires a direct reference in order to make sense. Whether these states are registered in language by the use of the word 'mind' is a trivial matter; less trivial is the category mistake of supposing that a person has a mind which is a substance independent of the body and the subject of predicates like those just discussed. Ryle called this the dogma of 'the Ghost in the Machine',[12] a phrase which has since become famous.

Indirect reference is not confined to talk of minds. People make choices and perform actions, but talk of 'the will' and its 'volitions' is no commentary on the mental performances which get the physical performances started. Marathon-runners may show exceptional determination to finish the course, and exclaim afterwards that it was only 'will power' that kept them going; but unfortunately there are no reserves of mental energy to switch over to when physical energy is used up, just more physical energy to be found from somewhere which comes, if at all, from reserves built up during training. People may want to report 'pangs of conscience', but would not know how to respond to the challenge to locate where the pangs were situated. 'Intelligence' and 'intellect' invite similar misclassification.[13] Such terms do not refer to things, yet they belong centrally to the way people speak about themselves and others. In so far as mentalistic terms refer, they refer to states of the person.

What I have called indirect reference is a type of realism akin to that worked out by Janet Martin Soskice in her *Metaphor and Religious Language*. P-predicates and mental-conduct words are not metaphors, and inasmuch as they are descriptions they describe not how the world is, but the states of human subjects. None the less there are several fruitful parallels. Metaphors, 'while not necessarily directly descriptive, may despite their limitations be reality depicting'.[14] The very vagueness of some metaphors may actually be a useful feature of them, for 'one can use terms to refer to little-understood features of the natural world without laying claim to unrevisable knowledge about them'.[15] And the reason why real reference is achievable by the use of metaphor is because, in the last analysis, 'It is not words which refer, but speakers using words who refer.'[16]

This account of indirect reference is substantiated by the later Wittgenstein. Followers of Wittgenstein who are interested in philosophy of religion have built up a large corpus of literature in the last twenty-five years, but they will not be followed here. The significance of many of Wittgenstein's insights for theology, especially his demolition of the Cartesian ego, is excitingly described by Fergus Kerr in his *Theology after Wittgenstein*.[17] For the present I want only to borrow from Wittgenstein's *Philosophical Investigations* two insights about the meaning of language. These are his remarks about the picture theory of meaning, and the difficulties which he puts in the way of supposing that there can be a private language which refers to inner states like pains, intentions, imaginings, and the like. The work begins with the rejection of Augustine's 'picture' of human language, in which 'the individual words in language name objects – sentences are combinations of such names'.[18] Wittgenstein comments, 'In this picture of language we find the roots of the following idea: Every word has a meaning. This meaning is correlated with the word. It is the object for which the word stands.' The picture theory is not entirely rejected, though. It is recognized as a very limited account of the meaning of language, and Wittgenstein shows that it cannot hold for many of the multifarious uses to which language is actually put,[19] especially for describing the various states which human beings undergo. According to a Cartesian view of mind and body, there are mental objects which come before 'the eye of the mind' that are analogous to physical objects which come before the eye of the body. The picture theory helps to sustain this mistaken view. Inner states and processes are thought to provide the unseen referents of talk about them, and we are thought to be able to name them because we have privileged private access to them. This is the view Wittgenstein wants to demolish when he sets up the question 'How do words *refer* to sensations? . . . how is the connexion between the name and the thing named set up?'[20]

There are several problems with a private-access theory. One concerns what is meant by a description. 'What we call *"descriptions"* are instruments for particular uses', uses which 'trick' us if we fail to notice the difference between '"I describe my state of mind" and "I describe my room"'.[21] Clearly there is a publicness, a checkability and an openness to observation about the latter which is absent from the former. Another problem about private language is the lack of attention to the public context necessary for language about one's states to be learned. A recurring example in the *Philosophical Investigations* is the attempt to describe the sensation of pain. If the expression 'I am in pain' gets its meaning from private sensations alone, then, says Wittgenstein, not only do 'I' generalize irresponsibly from my own case,[22] but I cannot expect to be understood when I announce my pain in public, for no public agreement about talk about pain would exist.

Wittgenstein's treatment of statements about pain may appear to have taken us far from the theme of the Person of Christ and the double languages which are spoken about him. Here, though, is a language which has a meaning and yet which is markedly unlike the descriptive language of everyday usage, which cannot be checked as everyday language can, yet is essential for self-expression and interpersonal understanding. Sensations are real but private, but the language used to describe them is publicly learned, with the result that the meaning of language cannot be derived from the sensations alone. We are likely to be misled, Wittgenstein tells us, if we construe 'the grammar of the expression of sensation on the model of "object and designation"'.[23] Sensations are indubitable, but they are not private pictures before the mind, any more than general psychological states like remembering, thinking and understanding are 'inner processes'.[24] That we are subjects of these sorts of experiences is not denied; only the sense of talk of inner processes and states is denied in any attempt to say more than can sensibly be said. So when states of a person are alluded to in language, the assumption of direct reference is badly misleading.

The third feature of P-predicates follows from the other two. They interpret the states of persons, in the first instance to themselves. Raziel Abelson (another supporter of complementarity) isolates two kinds of descriptions, both of which apply to persons but which do fundamentally different jobs and operate with different logical rules. These descriptions are physical and psychological, and they can easily be seen to correspond with Strawson's M- and P-predicates. What makes psychological descriptions differ from physical descriptions is their purpose. They explain and interpret the states of persons. Physical descriptions describe objects and events in the world and apply to a context where causal laws operate. Psychological descriptions refer to nothing in the world at all, for the job they do is not one of referring. Abelson holds that

> There are no purely mental objects, states, events or pro-
> cesses . . . Consequently it cannot be the job of psychological state-
> ments to refer to and describe and nomologically explain such *non*-
> entities. Insofar as psychological statements refer to anything, they must
> refer (but indirectly and vaguely) to bodily states and processes or tend-
> encies to such.

Abelson rightly denies that the function of psychological statements is to refer or describe; rather 'it is to interpret and evaluate
the states of agents, the actions toward which they incline, and the
circumstances that determine the moral or practical significance of
such states and actions'.[25]

Person language and the language of Christology compared

Let us now inquire whether these general features of person language are also features of the language of Christology. Clearly they
are. Christians have always wanted to say that in some sense Jesus
Christ was and is unique. Borrowing again from Chalcedon, let us
specify that of no other individual whatever could it be justly said
that he or she was 'of one substance with the Father' or 'like us in
all things apart from sin'. P-predicates are assignable to individuals
who are unique among other beings. The uniqueness of Jesus in
relation to other persons, a man without sin among sinful men and
women, is illuminated when it is compared with the uniqueness of
persons in the community of created beings. The comparison provides a starting-point for talking about uniqueness. Just as the person theory stipulates that persons are material beings whose
uniqueness requires them to be understood also as subjects of
P-predicates, so the Christian faith stipulates that the Person of
Christ is fully a human being, but one whose uniqueness among
human beings requires him to be understood as the subject of, we
might say, D- or deity predicates. A D-predicate is thus a predicate
which, when ascribed to Jesus of Nazareth, acknowledges his divinity. Human persons need P-predicates. The divine Person
needs D-predicates. All that is suggested at this stage is that a start
can be made towards filling out what is meant by the uniqueness of
Jesus by beginning with the uniqueness of persons among all the
beings God creates. The continuity and community which persons
have with the other creatures is the basis for noting the discontinuities which are also to be found. Likewise the Son of God
enters into a community and continuity with men and women,
and, on this basis, discontinuities are also to be found.

Second, the reference-relation between the divine subject and
the human predicates ascribed to it is, like the reference-relation
between the human subject and the mental-conduct words as-

cribed to it, real though indirect. What of 'religious-conduct words', like 'soul' and 'heart'? Do they refer? Is their meaning destroyed if they do not? They are of course indispensable to the language of spirituality, where 'soul', for example, has a sense in talk about the need for God, one's worth in the sight of God, one's relationship with God, and so on; and where 'heart' has a sense in talk about the centredness of a person (or lack of it), the deepest level of a person's being, and so on. 'Soul' and 'heart' refer, but to states of the person, not to things, so the reference-relation is odd.

Neither is this indirect reference-relation confined to states of the person, though it is with these that we are chiefly concerned at present. The terms 'heaven' and 'hell' may also be said genuinely to refer. Christians entertain the hope that since God is love he will confer eternal life upon them; equally, since God is just, they believe the final conquest of human wickedness may have punitive consequences. Popular pictures of heaven and hell doubtless at one time permitted believers to appropriate this belief in an imaginative and self-involving way; the same pictures, however, are likely today to provoke ridicule unless and until the reference-relation between the picture and what it pictures is loosened. There are real, though doubtless remote, referents in talk of heaven and hell, but their transtemporal reality is likely to be obscured when the detail of spatio-temporal description is insisted on. A similar remark may be made about one more set of examples, the 'last judgement' and 'the devil'. However the last judgement is depicted, it will be depicted as an event within time, yet it is the event which appraises the whole sum of human events and brings time itself to an end. Belief in Satan may be real testimony to the horrifying and invasive power of radical evil; once the popular picture of the devil is discarded, what was once pictured also gets discarded and the realistic assessment of the power of evil, its causes, instances and consequences, about which the Christian faith speaks clearly, is tragically lost.

The simple point about all these examples is that they have real though indirect referents. They can be tested against a correspondence theory of truth, provided any claimed correspondence is allowed to be appropriately tentative and loose-fitting. It is insufficient to use the terms 'myth', 'story', etc. in connection with them, because they often obfuscate the genuine claims about reality which religious language makes. All I am suggesting is that in the case of our own personal states we have immediate experience of what has been called 'indirect reference', and that similarities may be helpfully traced between indirect reference as an inescapable feature of 'person language' and indirect reference as an inescapable feature of religious language. In other words person language provides theology with a convenient precedent for loosening up the reference-relation while simultaneously providing an alternative interpretation of traditional terms. It also avoids reductionism, because it preserves the appropriate ontological level of the human subject.

The next example of ascription is that of Godhood. The language of Christology ascribes Godhood to Jesus. We can now carry forward from our previous discussion the conclusion that in person language P-predicates are ascribed to persons by means of common concepts such as mind, will and conscience, which do refer (though indirectly) to the states of persons (and so not to separate substances or things which persons are supposed to have). Now the language of Christology ascribes D-predicates to Jesus Christ. His deity or 'Godhood' is similarly not a separate substance or thing named by the term: it is the entire state of the incarnate Person Jesus Christ as the inclusive totality of divine and human natures. 'Godhood' is a real predication, yet, since we could say of no human being other than Jesus that he or she was God, we have here a case of unique language usage. The idea of indirect reference is most valuable in this connection, for, in accordance with the analogy based on person language, it enables us to make a profoundly meaningful claim about Jesus without expecting Godhood to be characterized by 'thinghood', and so conveniently defined and identified.

In this connection, by means of the analogical bridge which I have tried to build, Wittgenstein's remarks about the ascription of pain can be seen to have their application to christological statements too. Christians do not have private access to hidden knowledge about our Lord's divinity; there is no secret self-authentication or assurance about it that is conveniently inaccessible to the sceptical or scientific mind. The criteria for recognizing Godhood, like the criteria for learning a language, are public, and the early Church's growing recognition of the Godhood of Jesus doubtless included the entire Old Testament background together with the beliefs that Jesus was God's Servant, God's Son and God's Word. His ministry was utterly open to view, and was a matter of public controversy. What makes the unlikely comparison between the Church's ascription of Godhood to Jesus and Wittgenstein's discussion of the ascription of pain to an individual a surprisingly instructive one is that in both cases an ascription of a doubtful state to a person is intended. Wittgenstein's resolution of the sceptical doubt ('How do I know he really is in pain?') is to challenge the reasonableness of the doubt rather than to take the route of inference from the behaviour-state, which the observers see, to the pain-state, which they do not. I cannot experience another's pain, but I can be convinced of his or her pain by what I do experience of his behaviour, without having to make inferences

from one to the other. The ascription of Godhood to Jesus is
likewise non-inferential. Godhood was ascribed to Jesus not because it was an inference from what the earliest disciples experienced and believed, but precisely because it was present in
everything they experienced of Jesus, and because without this
crucial element in their account of this experience the account
would be incomplete.

When Christians claim that 'Jesus is God the Son' they *do* intend
a description, but it is unavoidable, as Wittgenstein has reminded
us, that 'what we call "descriptions" are instruments for particular
uses', and the 'particular use' for which the language of Christology is employed is strictly unparalleled. It is more like 'I describe
my state of mind' than 'I describe my room', but it is also unlike
both. But the parallel holds at the point at which we ask how each
kind of description can be checked. P-predicates and D-predicates
are checkable, though they are clearly not checkable in the same
way observation-statements are. 'Just try – in a real case – to doubt
someone else's fear or pain', observes Wittgenstein.[26] If a person,
in self-ascribing, is telling the truth, his or her behaviour will be
consistent with what he/she says. And, inadequate though the over-
used term 'behaviour' may be in relation to the life of Christ, we
may say that it was the very witnessing of his behaviour, and the
disciples' mature reflection upon it, which so strikingly confirmed
his Godhood in the first place. God became publicly recognizable
because he became known in the life and actions of Jesus.

Theologians and philosophers of religion who have interested
themselves in religious language have not always been fully aware
of the possibilities involved in modelling religious language on person language. At the present time, though, it is more widely accepted that much religious language is not to be as literally interpreted
as once it was. This is a gain for theology. But once the literal
element of some theological discourse is somewhat toned down,
what fills the vacuum? Some writers say that theological language
must be understood as mythology, poetry, etc., for it is suggested
that in myth and poetry there is an obvious loosening up of the
relationship between language and its referent, and this is what a
modern theory of religious language requires. If the argument of
the present chapter can be sustained, religious language is better
compared with person language than with the language of poetry
and myth, for here, in the very discourse we use about ourselves,
we come across a paradigm case of language which both confers
meaning on our actions while at the same time retaining the ontological fullness of the person without reduction. What we have
called person language does have a referent (in ourselves); yet the
reference is indirect. I think there are gains to be made by modelling at least some theological language on person language rather

than on the language of poetry and myth, for the latter discounts the ontological realism which is essential for maintaining both the distinctiveness of persons among created beings and the distinctiveness of the Person of Christ among persons.

The divine Word: the personalization of God

Finally, in bringing the comparison between person language and christological language to a close, we may claim the language of Christology interprets Jesus as God, and so its logic may be fruitfully compared with Abelson's account of psychological language. As we have seen, Abelson is slightly ambivalent about whether psychological descriptions do or do not refer, but since he claims their main task is interpretation the question is unimportant. As psychological descriptions 'interpret and evaluate' the states of human agents, so the names and titles of Jesus 'interpret and evaluate' his being, his actions and his significance. The very designation of Jesus Christ as God's Word or Logos provides a fine illustration of the overlap between christological and person language, and in fact it draws on all three features mentioned above. The background to the Logos poem in John 1 includes Philo and the Stoics, where the 'basic meaning' of the concept is 'thought, reason' and 'speech, utterance'.[27] The two types of *logos*, writes James D. G. Dunn, were the unexpressed thought (the *logos endiathetos*) and the *logos* expressed in speech (the *logos prophorikos*). Immediately, then, it is clear that the meaning of the application of the term *logos* to God's incarnate presence in Jesus Christ, whatever its background, derives from a context of human self-consciousness. It has already been noted that the entertaining of thoughts and their articulation in speech is something done only by persons, and that they interpret the personal states of the utterer. Jesus did not as far as we know regard himself as the Word of God and so did not use the term in the sense intended by the writer of the Johannine prologue. However, the term has had an immense influence on the development of Christology; indeed 'Logos christology served as a crucial phase in early Christianity's attempts to explain itself to *itself*, to come to a coherent understanding and statement of its faith concerning Christ.'[28] Here the parallel is between P-predicates and D-predicates, both of which interpret the states of persons. In one case P-predicates interpret and evaluate the states and actions of human agents; in the other case the believing community ascribes D-predicates to Jesus in its attempt to interpret his life, death and resurrection in its totality.

The parallel may be pressed further. Dunn reminds us that in the Old Testament God's Word, like God's Wisdom and God's Spirit, sometimes appears as if it were an independent person. Such an impression is of course misleading, because it confuses personification with personalization.[29] All three terms turn out to be 'variant ways of speaking of the creative, revelatory or redemptive act of God'. Once again Ryle's warning against category mistakes is timely, for to speak of God's Word is not to speak of something in a category apart from God but is to speak of God in his action towards humankind in Jesus. Wittgenstein's remarks about naming and describing could hardly be more apposite than they are in the present context, for here we have immensely important names whose relation to the bearer of those names is not what we might expect. As mental-conduct terms have their indirect reference in the states of persons, so these theological terms have their indirect reference in the states of the one personal God, and particularly in God's activity toward the world. We may also note that the difficulties in a straightforward referential interpretation of the term are not sufficient to justify the classification of the divine Word-become-flesh as mythological. There is no historical evidence for Bultmann's suggestion, claims Dunn, that behind the Logos poem of John 1 there lies a 'pre-Christian Gnostic myth'.[30] And we have given theological reasons for insisting that if we play down the literal and directly referential interpretation of theological terms we are not required to substitute myth and poetry as alternative paradigms of meaning. Person language provides a superior model.

The most striking resemblance between person language and the language of Christology lies in what Dunn calls 'the astounding nature', 'the revolutionary significance' of the claims about the Logos in John 1.[31] Only in the statement 'So the Word became flesh; he came to dwell among us . . .' is the 'huge leap' made from the personification of God in his Word, Wisdom and Spirit to the identification of God with a human person. John 1.14, then, brings to expression that re-casting of the logical rules of Christian talk of God.[32] The term 'Word of God' before and after Jesus undergoes a profound change in its meaning. After Jesus the term comes to acquire a historical, personal referent. After the Church reflects for half a century or so on her faith in the crucified and risen Jesus, the logical rules governing what is to count as 'God' are slowly altered, until in the Gospel of John they are daringly laid down, to be further developed in subsequent centuries. What is primarily, though not of course exclusively, to be understood by 'God' has now been made explicit: Jesus Christ. Christians today no longer have the benefit of a background in Palestinian and Alexandrian Judaism, Hellenism and Stoicism, and so may well wonder whether the Logos concept is sound linguistic currency any longer. I think the position here is akin to the post-Cartesian use of 'mind'. If reflective talk about minds aims at combating reductive theories of persons, so be it. The ontology must be protected somehow, and – provided no dualism is intended – talk of 'mind' still has its uses.

The essential ontology of the Christian faith is that what is meant by 'God' is found in the being of Jesus of Nazareth – God has become truly and completely man. Whether the ontology must be expressed by means of the Logos concept is a secondary matter.

The divine Word, then, is the personalization of God through Jesus.The next chapter will discuss the 'I am' sayings of Jesus, where Godhood is not simply ascribed to Jesus by the Church but is self-ascribed by Jesus himself. And the work we have done on person language in this chapter will enable us to take a fresh look at the meaning of the 'I am' sayings.

NOTES

1 M. F. Wiles, 'A Reply to Mr Baelz' in S. W. Sykes and J. P. Clayton (eds), *Christ, Faith and History* (Cambridge: Cambridge University Press, 1972), p. 36.

2 Gilbert Ryle, *The Concept of Mind* (Harmondsworth: Penguin Books, 1976, 1st pub. 1949), pp. 17–18.

3 ibid., p. 17.

4 ibid., p. 10.

5 M. F. Wiles, 'Does Christology Rest on a Mistake?' in Sykes and Clayton, *Christ, Faith and History*, p. 11 emphasis added.

6 Ryle, *The Concept of Mind*, p. 13, p. 10.

7 Wiles, 'Does Christology Rest on a Mistake?', p. 12.

8 *Mind*, xxi (1912), rep. H. A. Prichard, *Moral Obligation* (Oxford: Oxford University Press, 1949).

9 I agree with Morris that the incarnation provides 'certain presuppositions or controls' within which theologians must operate. But I do not think his dubious distinction between full humanity and mere humanity can be derived from them: therein lies the danger of making a special appeal to revelation. See Thomas V. Morris, *The Logic of God Incarnate* (Ithaca and London: Cornell University Press, 1986), p. 64, and above, ch. 4.

10 Ryle, *The Concept of Mind*, p. 17.

11 ibid. p. 18.

12 ibid. p. 17.

13 ibid., ch. 2.

14 Janet Martin Soskice, *Metaphor and Religious Language* (Oxford: Clarendon Press, 1985), p. 136.

15 ibid., p. 134.

16 ibid., p. 136.

17 Fergus Kerr, *Theology after Wittgenstein* (Oxford: Basil Blackwell, 1986). Kerr's book is especially significant in showing the damage done to theology by 'mentalist/individualist' theories of the person and how Wittgenstein's philosophy can help to overcome it. Kerr warns that 'In all traditions, Christian theologians are to be found who work with a concept of the self that needs to go to the cleaners . . .' (p. 187). I hope he won't find the one I am employing too tatty!

18 L. Wittgenstein, *Philosophical Investigations*, tr. G. E. M. Anscombe (Oxford: Basil Blackwell, 1972; 1st pub. 1953). §1.

19 ibid., §3, *et seq.*

20 ibid., §244.

21 ibid., §290.

22 ibid., §293.

23 ibid.

24 ibid., §339.
25 Raziel Abelson, *Persons* (London and Basingstoke: Macmillan, 1977), p. 13.
26 Wittgenstein, *Philosophical Investigations*, §303.
27 James D. G. Dunn, *Christology in the Making* (London: S C M Press, 1980), p. 223.
28 ibid.' p. 213.
29 ibid., p. 219.
30 ibid., p. 215, p. 262.
31 ibid., p. 243.
32 ibid., p. 27, *et seq.*

CHAPTER 6

Jesus – God in Person

In the present chapter the analogy between the human person and the divine Person enters a new phase. The direction of the analogy from persons to the divine Person of Christ remains, while the content begins with the meaning of the pronoun 'I' and moves towards the meaning of the divine 'I' on the lips of Jesus. The name of God revealed to Moses in Exodus 3.14 is 'I AM'. The Christology of the fourth Gospel deliberately ascribes the divine name 'I AM' to Jesus. The 'I am' sayings are one of the ways the author depicts Jesus' Godhood. An analogy between the human 'I' and the divine 'I' will illuminate what is involved in doing so. In the first part of this chapter the biblical material will be described. Next, three philosophical themes of obvious relevance to the interpretation of the 'I am' sayings are introduced. These are naming, self-ascription or 'avowal', and personal identity. These topics are the philosophical materials out of which the analogy between the human and divine 'I's is built. The ambitious conclusions to be worked towards are that through Jesus Christ, the bearer of God's name, God-in-person literally tells us who he is and what he does. Jesus self-ascribes his own divinity, and the 'I' which self-ascribes is a single divine/human 'I'. But the positing of a single divine/human 'I' cannot fail to raise questions about the being of the subject posited, in particular how the 'I' on the lips of Jesus can be both a divine and a human subject, while remaining also a *single* subject. Chapters 7 and 8 provide a fresh approach to this problem. The issue of the relation between the divine Personhood of Christ and his human nature is discussed there.

The name of God and the 'I am' sayings of Jesus

Theologians down the centuries have been fascinated by the 'I AM' name of God and have discovered meanings in the Exodus text which the text itself could not begin to support. According to the book of Exodus, when Moses receives his call from God at the burning bush he asks God:

'If I go to the Israelites and tell them that the God of their forefathers has sent me to them, and they ask me his name, what shall I say?' God answered, 'I AM'; that is who I am. Tell them that I AM has sent you to them.' And God said further, 'You must tell the Israelites this, that it is

JEHOVAH the God of their forefathers, the God of Abraham, the God of Isaac, the God of Jacob, who has sent you to them. This is my name for ever; this is my title in every generation.' (Exodus 3.13–15).

As the text stands the words spoken by God are intended as an interpretation of the name 'Jehovah', which (in the J tradition of the Pentateuch) is a name for God from Genesis 2 onwards. The key words 'I AM; that is who I am' are sometimes rendered 'I will be what I will be' (see the marginal note in the New English Bible). The verb *hayah* expresses actual phenomenal being, so it would be a mistake to find in these words a doctrine of absolute existence. The present tense can easily convey the impression of abstract timelessness (as the Septuagint's rendering *ego eimi ho on* suggests), whereas the alternative future tense rendering might be thought to emphasize Jehovah's active historical existence. The Hebrew 'Jehovah' derives from the same root as *ehyeh*, which gives rise to the English alternatives 'I am', 'I will be'. If the future tense is adopted, then the words express the promise to Moses and the Israelites that Jehovah will be what he will be. Of course just what Jehovah will be is open-ended and undefined; only subsequent history will reveal it. If the present tense is retained, then, as we shall see, Moses is given a lesson in the 'non-objectifiability' of God. The alternative account of Moses' call in Exodus 6 has God saying three times to Moses 'I am the LORD' (Exodus 6.2–8). There the revelation of the divine name Jehovah is given along with the promise to the Israelites that they will be rescued from slavery, adopted as God's people and led to the promised land. Moses is to report to the people: 'I will release you . . . I will rescue you . . . I will redeem you . . . I will become your God.' As a result of the promised actions, God says, 'You shall know that I, the LORD, am your God, the God who releases you from your labours in Egypt.'

The 'I am' sayings in the fourth Gospel must be understood in the light of the name of Jehovah and the illuminating words 'I AM; that is who I am.' Raymond Brown thinks that by the time of Deutero-Isaiah 'I AM' was used as a divine name, so that 'against this background the absolute use of *ego eimi* ['I am'] becomes quite intelligible. Jesus is presented as speaking in the same manner in which Yahweh speaks in Deutero-Isaiah.'[1] In Deutero-Isaiah Yahweh chooses his servant Israel 'that you may know and believe me and understand that *ego eimi*' (Isaiah 43.10). There are four instances of the absolute use of 'I am' in the Gospel of John.[2] The first of these is John 8.24, where Jesus says. 'If you do not believe that *ego eimi*, you will die in your sins.' The absoluteness is underlined by the characteristic incomprehension of the Jews in the fourth Gospel who ask 'Who are you?' wrongly thinking that Jesus had failed to give his name. The clearest expression of our Lord's divinity in the Gospels is the saying in John 8.58 where the evangelist describes how Jesus tells the Jews 'In very truth I tell you, before Abraham was born, *ego eimi*.' The response ('They picked up stones to throw at him') indicated the Jews well understood what was meant. Jesus is either the authentic bearer of the name of God or a blasphemer against it; an offence deserving blasphemy (Leviticus 24.16).

Jesus is therefore commended in the fourth Gospel as the bearer of God's name. Another group of sayings links 'I am' with a nominative predicate. Jesus says 'I am the bread of life'; 'I am the light of the world'; 'I am the door of the sheepfold'; 'I am the good shepherd'; 'I am the resurrection and I am life'; 'I am the way; I am the truth and I am life'; and 'I am the real vine'.[3] In these statements the affirmation of our Lord's divinity is combined with a series of predicates which describe

> what he is in relation to man. In his mission Jesus is the source of eternal life for men ('vine', 'life', 'resurrection'); he is the means through whom men find life ('way', 'gate'); he leads men to life ('shepherd'); he reveals to men the truth ('truth') which nourishes their life ('bread').[4]

Some of the 'I am' sayings, then, declare what Jesus *is*; others declare what Jesus *does*.[5]

The biblical 'I am' sayings are remarkable for many reasons. They are associated in the Old Testament with God's revelation to the Israelites and his intervention on their behalf; in the New Testament the sayings reveal the real identity of Jesus. A principal feature of anyone being a person is the ability to adopt what is called, grammatically, a 'first-person' perspective upon oneself. This is described shortly. The revelatory words to Moses already presuppose that God is a subject of first-person ascriptions. Jehovah among gods, like a person among non-persons, is a transcending subject. We might speculate that no ordinary personification is going on here, for if the writer had wished only to personify God simpler formulations were available to him which are in fact used throughout the Old Testament. All that is suggested so far is that the stage is set for the ascription of P-predicates to God, for God is revealed as a transcending subject of P-predicates. 'I AM' is therefore not to be taken as a P-predicate, as if God were ascribing to himself an absolute existence; rather we may say the text provides the preconditions for the possibility of certain P-predicates being ascribed to God. In so far as God is identified by the name 'I AM', he is identified as an active personal subject.

The self-ascription of Godhood

The character of the divine subject may be illuminated by asking the philosophical question 'What happens when a subject is named?' Moses asks God for a name, because he will need to

identify the source of the theophany when he declares himself the
leader of the Israelites. The request is refused, or at any rate not
answered as Moses wished. God is 'I AM', and Moses has to tell the
suspicious Israelites that 'I AM has sent you to them'. This is an
unpromising opening gambit! Its apparent unintelligibility has ever
since been a challenge exegetes have been unable to resist. Local
deities all had names – without names no prayers or sacrifices
would be possible. The God of Israel, however, cannot even begin
to be compared with these gods. Wittgenstein's masterly under-
mining of the reference theory of naming in the *Philosophical Investigations* will help us to recover the sense of dramatic encounter
between Moses and God which the Exodus narrative conveys.

In the course of his attack on logical atomism Wittgenstein remarks that

> It is important to note that the word 'meaning' is being used illicitly if it
> is used to signify the thing that 'corresponds' to the word. That is to
> confound the meaning of a name with the *bearer* of the name. When Mr
> M.N. dies one says that the bearer of the name dies, not that the mean-
> ing dies.[6]

If, then, Moses expects some god to correspond to the revealed
name, he is in for a big disappointment, for the bearer of the name
'I AM' does not correspond to the name as a simple reference
theory of meaning suggests. God cannot be named because he is
no ordinary bearer of a name, and to that extent cannot be recognized, apprehended or identified. 'Moses covered his face, for he
was afraid to gaze on God' (Exodus 3.6). According to the over-
simple reference theory of meaning, the act of naming a person
requires some sort of correspondence between the name and the
person. This is precisely what Moses cannot have, for he does not
know who is speaking to him or what corresponds to 'I AM'. Moses
has to reckon from the beginning with the absolute subjectness of
God. God is a personal subject and must therefore be a real object
both to Moses and to all men and women who experience him. But
while 'I AM' conveys a real reference, its real reference is also
beyond Moses' comprehension, and therefore casts doubt on the
adequacy of standard word-referent or name-bearer relations
which bring it into language. Theologically, the point is simple.
God's name is above every name, a distinction which an early
Christian hymn ascribes to Jesus (Philippians 2.9).

In John's Gospel Jesus clearly ascribes Godhood to himself, and
it is of the utmost importance to consider what is going on when
human self-ascriptions are made, before we move on to discussing
the momentous self-ascriptions of Jesus Christ. The discussion of
P-predicates in earlier chapters did not distinguish between self-
ascription and other-ascription; this must now be done. The dis-

tinction may also help to ease the vexed problem of the historicity of the 'I am' sayings. Strawson insists that it is essential to the character of P-predicates 'that they have both first- and third-person ascriptive uses, that they are both self-ascribable otherwise than on the basis of observation of the behaviour of the subject of them, and other-ascribable on the basis of behaviour criteria'.[7] In practice, then, the third-person statement 'He is tired' contains a P-predicate made, say, on the basis of observing him yawn, whereas the first-person statement 'I am tired' does not express an observation about myself at all; it just reports the way I feel. The point to carry forward to the theological exegesis of the 'I am' sayings is the obvious one that P-predicates are of two kinds. They are ascribable to other persons on the basis of observation, and they are ascribable to oneself without observation. The 'I am' sayings as they appear in the Bible belong exclusively to the second sort; they are self-ascriptions.

This simple insistence on self-ascription, together with the first-person perspective which we have already noted in connection with 'I AM; that is who I am', introduces a new and important element into christological discussion. When the complementary language thesis is applied to the life of Christ in the way Robinson tries to do, there are only different third-person perspectives to take up in relation to it. Both stories he wants to tell make the Christ firmly the object, that which presents double aspects. But what must not be lost, I aver, is the first-person perspective of Jesus upon himself. I do not mean by this another attempt to speculate about the self-consciousness of Jesus by means of inference from the historically more reliable bits of the Gospels. I mean that if we take the biblical 'I am' sayings somewhat as modern philosophers take self-ascriptions, a new approach to the Godhood of Jesus is possible. But that is to anticipate. Taking seriously the first-person perspective of Jesus upon himself also enables us to claim that the principle of complementarity is being used as a genuine truth-conveying method, for as we have seen,[8] a person's self-consciousness is what makes complementarity applicable to persons initially.

Avowals – human and divine

Avowals, or self-ascriptions, therefore constitute a class of discourse which might have particular significance for theology, so it is necessary to summarize what is going on when avowals are made. Ryle remarks (in a phrase which bursts with theological applicability) that an avowal is an act of 'voluntary non-concealment'.[9] In ascribing to oneself a feeling or a state, one does not proclaim the result of an investigation any more than one establishes something by evidence or infers it from clues.[10] Ryle's examples of avowals seem to be chosen for their triviality: feeling bored, cheerful or tired, announcing that one has a tickle, and so on. But other writers have shown the centrality of avowals both in general conversation and in human self-understanding. Abelson thinks it is 'a little-noticed fact that *all psychological knowledge* is erected upon a foundation of first-person, present-tense, self-descriptions'.[11] We might add that even the Chalcedonian definition is an avowal, for it begins with the words 'We all with one voice confess . . .' Avowals 'are our unique way of making public the states of which we have non-observational self-knowledge'.[12] They do not merely bring to the surface trivial feeling-states – they include first-person statements about 'thinking, believing, loving, wanting'.[13] They announce people's *reasons* for their actions, whereas finding *causes* for actions involves a different set of descriptions. The former is first-person psychological explanation; the latter third-person causal explanation.[14] Avowals are 'incorrigible' in that they are 'not normally subject to challenge'.[15] 'Not normally' allows for cases of hallucination, deception, etc. Avowals are checkable. We might come to mistrust someone who said he was concerned about poverty yet did nothing to alleviate it; or who claimed to be a socialist while subscribing to private health insurance. According to Ryle the test-question to ask in suspicious cases is 'Sincere or shammed?'[16]

A person, then, may make an avowal without observation, without evidence, and normally without challenge. We may observe that the promises made to Moses are avowals. In saying 'I will release you . . .' God declares his intentions for Israel, because true public intentions are avowals. Jehovah is not seen, there is no evidence that the Israelites are about to escape, and the words are accepted without challenge. Indeed even the words 'I am Jehovah' constitute a kind of avowal, an avowal of trustworthiness, akin to 'Because I am Jehovah I am trustworthy'. The declaration 'assures the reader that what is stated has divine authority and comes from God'.[17] It is a sufficient indication of the authority of the promises. Trust in the God who promises leads to knowledge, and this knowledge confirms (we might say) that the test-question 'Sincere or shammed?' is about to be answered affirmatively.

St John reports Jesus as avowing 'I am the light of the world'. This is an avowal which *is* challenged. The Pharisees think the claim is shammed, and they think this because they think the avowal should rest on evidence, whereas in their view it does not. Their charge is 'You are witness in your own cause [lit. 'You witness concerning yourself']; your testimony is not valid' (John 8.13). In his reply Jesus makes no attempt to conceal the lack of independent testimony, but uses it as a demonstration, for those who will have faith, of his having come from the Father. 'My testimony is valid, even though I do bear witness about myself;

because I know where I come from, and where I am going' (8.14). The two witnesses which Jesus provides in accordance with the law of testimony are his own witness 'concerning myself' (*peri emautou*) and 'the Father who sent me' (8.18). The New English Bible makes it clear that the Pharisees do not even realize that Jesus is referring to his heavenly Father, for their question 'Where is your father?' has 'father' in lower case. Jesus' reply re-identifies himself with God – 'You know neither me nor my Father; if you knew me you would know my Father as well' (8.19).

I add to standard discussions of this passage the observation that a whole class of utterances are made by persons which, while challengeable, can reasonably be believed by others without evidence. Jesus' testimony 'concerning myself' is in principle as incorrigible as my testimony that I dreamed last night about my holiday and that I will play tennis on Tuesday. Of course John's Gospel is full of material intended as evidence that Jesus comes from God, yet in the end Jesus is bound to be put in the impossible position of being his own witness for no one else could know in advance what it would be like for someone both to come from God and to be God unless they too had come from God and were God. If Jesus is uniquely God, then no third-person perspective, i.e. that of witnesses, can in principle establish it, for no one would in the last resort know what they were looking for. (Even the witness of John the Baptist to Jesus is made to rest on a direct revelation to John (John 1.32–4).) But plenty of people claim to have come from God – how do we sort out Jesus from the rest? To ask this question is to ask whether his witness in his own cause is sincere or shammed. Jesus is 'I am'. But for those who believe this, the gospel writer produces a mass of evidence which corroborates the basic belief 'that Jesus is the Christ, the Son of God, and that through this faith you may possess life *by his name*' (John 20.31, italics added). So faith in Jesus as God's Son is no blind, *blik*-like trust,[18] but a considered personal response to God's identification of himself through a person, to which the signs of Jesus, the testimony of others, and his life, death and resurrection all bear witness.

Jesus – the personal identity of God

Let us now turn to the logical subject of the 'I am' sayings. A useful starting-point here is Wittgenstein's remark that '"I" is not the name of a person, nor "here" of a place, and "this" is not a name. But they are connected with names. Names are explained by means of them.'[19] When a person makes an avowal the use of 'I' does not stand for that person's name. We may also rule out two other alternatives which have their supporters, the 'mental substance' (or 'inner substance') theory and, following Hume, the 'bundle' theory. Dualists and materialists alike hold versions of a

substance theory, for they both try to locate the substance to which
'I' refers, the former arguing for a mental substance[20] and the latter
for a wholly material one. Hume, on the other hand, despaired of
finding a referent for 'I', concluding that we 'are nothing but a
bundle or collection of different perceptions, which succeed each
other with an inconceivable rapidity, and are in a perpetual flux
and movement'.[21] However, we are not obliged to take sides in the
argument whether personal identity consists in body, mind or anything else. A more plausible position, and the one adopted in this
book, is that a person is a unitary substance comprising body and
mind (but the term 'entity' has generally been preferred). Persons
are entities which can ascribe P-predicates to themselves without
observation and to other persons on the basis of observation. The
reference problem attaching to the use of 'I' is solved for Strawson
by eliminating both 'the pure subject' and the material body as
candidates for the reference and substituting 'person' for both. 'I'
does refer. This is 'because I am a person among others; and the
predicates which would, *per impossibile* belong to the pure subject if
it could be referred to, belong properly to the person to which "I"
does refer'.[22] This is of course no solution to the personal identity
problem, but is the consistent denial that, from the premises on
which the person theory is built, there is a problem to solve.

The notion of indirect reference was explored in the last chapter,
and its application is clearly appropriate here. Let us say that when
one says 'I', one refers non-trivially but indirectly to 'the person I
am' (and so neither to body, nor to mind, nor to a bundle of
perceptions, nor to nothing at all). Let us now return to the 'I am'
sayings. The crucial difference between God's 'I AM; that is who I
am', addressed to Moses, and the use of *ego eimi* on the lips of
Jesus, addressed to his disciples, is that while the divine subject
appears only indirectly to Moses, in Jesus the divine subject appears in person. The precise meaning of 'person' here is discussed
in chapters 7 and 8. One distinction between direct and indirect
reference can be particularly significant when placed within a discussion about divine revelation. The unseen Jehovah promises to
intervene in the events of history and to become disclosed through
his actions. The divine subject makes himself known through theophany, the law and the prophets, through his servant. But the
divine subject is 'systematically elusive'.[23] So far there is no revelation in a person, though there is much personification. But on the
lips of a human being, the divine name 'I AM' at last gets a literal
referent. God-in-person speaks. God-in-person *is* the subject of
'before Abraham was born, I am' (John 8.58). God no longer
needs personification, because God is now disclosed as a person.
For the first time, the meaning of the name and the bearer of the
name are indissolubly brought together. One might even say (with

half a glance towards recent controversy) that the incarnation is the end of myth, instead of an instance of myth, for it finally gives the unseen God a personal referent and abolishes speculation once and for all about who he is.

This conclusion is important. A contrast which may illustrate further the difference between the 'I am' sayings of the Old and New Testaments is that just used, between the bundle of different perceptions which Hume ruefully suggested might stand for 'I' and the person theory where 'I' refers to 'the person I am'. But the illustration provides only a subsidiary analogy with limited elucidatory power. On each side of the analogy an elusive subject is sought and a transformation brought about in the means of finding it. On the philosophical side of the analogy the subject sought is the elusive unknown self, and a transition is made from Hume's scepticism, where the self is no more than a bundle of perceptions, to the 'person theory', where the person is an ontological subject transcending the mind/body divide. On the theological side the subject sought is the elusive pre-incarnational God of the Old Testament and the transition made is from the incomplete and fragmentary Old Testament revelation to the complete and final revelation of God in Jesus. It is possible, without dismissiveness, to regard the theophanies of the Old Testament also as a 'bundle of different perceptions', this time perceptions of God. The point of doing this is solely to draw attention to the lack of an identifiable personal referent in the tradition, and Hume's phrase successfully achieves this. God's actions are mediated through prophets, the law, theophanies, miracles, historical events, and so on. God is worshipped through personal acts and is richly personified as the tradition develops. But he is unseen, elusive and only identified as that which is unidentifiable. By contrast, incarnational faith holds that God is now seen, unelusive (even nailed to a cross) and explicitly identifiable. Christians will not therefore easily abandon what they take as a once-for-all revelation of God for a general concept of the divine which gets loosely (if at all) tied to the human Jesus. Incarnational faith is, to pursue the parallel a little further, a substance theory, just as the person theory is. Both in fact enlarge our category of substance. The tradition of the God of Moses and the patriarchs now gives us God in his very being.

Jesus and the publicness of God

Being a person includes having the ability to ascribe states, feelings, intentions, reasons and the like to oneself without observation. These are avowals. The person Jesus of Nazareth also made avowals, some of which are recorded in the Gospels. In some of these the single logical subject is both Jesus of Nazareth and God-in-person. St John's explicit ascription of the divine name to Jesus allows Jesus to speak not merely *for* God, as his Messiah, but *as* God, the Son of the Father. Following the characteristics of avowals set out in this chapter, Jesus, we may say, is God's act of voluntary non-concealment. God makes public through Jesus his promises, feelings, thoughts, and loving purposes, etc. In the purely human case avowals are the means of making public such matters. In the case of God, Jesus is the means of making public such matters, and now of course not merely the utterances of Jesus (including within them the tiny class of 'I am' sayings) are meant but that totality which is his earthly life.

I have not discussed the historicity of the 'I am' sayings. Perhaps John is faithful to the Markan tradition, where at his trial Jesus again says *ego eimi*, and is unanimously convicted of blasphemy (Mark 14.61–4). The problem of historicity is thought by some theologians to undermine completely the doctrine of the incarnation.[24] There is scarcely a single competent New Testament scholar who is prepared to defend the view that the four instances of the absolute use of 'I am' in John, or indeed most of the other uses, can be historically attributed to Jesus, and I have no wish to quarrel with that general verdict. The original conversation between Moses and God is even more obviously a candidate for historical scepticism. Faced with this dilemma, acutely felt by biblical theologians, one might arm oneself with the convenient distinction between historical fact and theological interpretation and claim that John must have had historical reasons for making his theological judgements. We would then be back with the 'two stories' of Wiles and Robinson.[25] But now another obvious problem arises: the gap between what Jesus may have said and what subsequent biblical writers say he said may have become so wide that the theological judgements are historically unsupportable. At this juncture the distinction between self-ascription and other-ascription becomes useful.

P-predicates are a class of predicates which include both self-ascription and other-ascription. But, in accordance with the logical rules governing P-predicates, each kind is possible only within a community of individuals which recognizes that each member is a person. Now let us assume the standard view that the 'I am' sayings are unhistorical. What follows, in accordance with the distinction, is the conclusion that what were hitherto believed to be self-ascriptions turn out to be other-ascriptions, ascriptions by the Church to Jesus. At least one can say that the observations on the basis of which the ascriptions are made are well-founded. Jesus was literally and physically a member of the community of the disciples – the writer of 1 John can even say of the revelation of God in Jesus that 'we looked upon it, and we felt it with our own hands' (1 John 1.1). The other-ascriptions are historically well-grounded. But if the all-important self-ascriptions turn out to be only other-ascriptions, products of the believing community, isn't the case for regarding the 'I am' sayings as the self-identification of God-in-person fatally weakened?

Weakened, yes, but not fatally. The method of this study is, in any case, illustration, not demonstration, and the 'I am' sayings have been chosen in the present chapter because of their considerable illustrative power in developing the basic series of analogies from the human person to the divine/human Person of Christ. The series itself does not fall if the standard historical judgement about the 'I am' sayings is upheld. However, the practice of separating historical facts from theological judgements must not be allowed to dismantle altogether the possibility that through the phenomenal events that lie at the roots of the gospel narrative God is none the less becoming revealed. If on reading John's Gospel a reader became convinced that Jesus Christ was God-in-person, that is surely what the author of that Gospel would have us believe. John did not have our modern concept of 'fact'. Perhaps our modern worry about the historicity of the 'I am' sayings, and of countless other sayings attributed to Jesus, should be countered by another worry – that the dominance since the Enlightenment of the rigid distinction between fact and value may be causing us to lose sight of the very values which in the biblical record have been skilfully combined with what are now called 'facts'. Theologians must not be enticed by the simplistic distinctions between facts and values or events and interpretations. Alasdair MacIntyre convincingly shows that 'facts, like telescopes and wigs for gentlemen, were a seventeenth-century invention'.[26] 'Fact', he reminds us, translates *factum*, 'something done', and is therefore inseparable from purpose. Once the 'I am' sayings are construed as a possible but highly unlikely series of historical 'facts' ripped away from the settled purpose of the Gospel which gives its content meaning, then perhaps their theological importance is irrecoverable. (Elsewhere I have attempted a sketch of an epistemology which tries to get behind the fact-value divide.)[27]

Were there then two 'I's? Complementarity will again be shown to come to our aid. The divine 'I' and the human 'I' are identical. The single holy mystery which is the being of the incarnate Lord must be approached in complementary ways. The divine/human subject requires us to speak of both a human 'I' and a divine 'I', without positing two persons in the one Son. So far, when I have referred to the humanity of Jesus I have avoided using the concept of human person of him, using always 'Person' to stand for the single divine subject of his divine and human natures. His humanity has been variously referred to as 'man', 'a man', 'a human being', etc. Can it now be maintained that, in order to defend his real solidarity with *human* persons, we may speak of his being a *human* person, too? If we could do so, would we strengthen his co-humanity with us, or damage the analogy between the human person and the divine Person which has so far been built up? This issue cannot be postponed any longer and will therefore be taken up in the next chapter.

NOTES

1 Raymond Brown, *The Gospel According to John* vol. i (London: Geoffrey Chapman, 1971), pp. 536–7.
2 ibid., p. 533.
3 John 6.35,51; 8.12(9.5); 10.7,9; 10.11,14; 11.25; 14.6; 15.1,5.
4 Brown, *The Gospel According to John* vol. 1, p. 534.
5 For a fuller classification and description of the sayings, see Brown, ibid., Appendix 4, pp. 533–8.
6 L. Wittgenstein, *Philosophical Investigations*. tr. G. E. M. Anscombe (Oxford: Basil Blackwell, 1972, 1st pub. 1953), §40.
7 P. F. Strawson, *Individuals* (London: Methuen, 1959), p. 108.
8 Above. pp. 40–3.
9 Gilbert Ryle, *The Concept of Mind* (Harmondsworth: Penguin Books, 1976, 1st pub. 1949), p. 99.
10 ibid., p. 98.
11 Raziel Abelson, *Persons* (London and Basingstoke: Macmillan, 1977), p. 13, emphasis added. See his Introduction and chs 1 and 2 for an extensive analysis of avowals.
12 ibid., p. 27.
13 ibid., p. 6.
14 ibid., p. 10
15 ibid., p. 24.
16 Ryle, *The Concept of Mind*, p. 99.
17 Brown, *The Gospel According to John* vol i, p. 536.
18 On *bliks* and their unshakeable character, see R. M. Hare in ch. 1 of B. Mitchell (ed.), *The Philosophy of Religion* (Oxford: Oxford University Press, 1971).
19 Wittgenstein, *Philosophical Investigations*, §410.
20 Above, p. 19.
21 David Hume, *A Treatise of Human Nature* (1739) Oxford: Oxford University Press, ²1978), p. 252.
22 Strawson, *Individuals*, p. 103.
23 A phrase of Ryle's about the pronoun 'I': Ryle, *The Concept of Mind*, p. 178.
24 e.g. Maurice Wiles, *The Remaking of Christian Doctrine* (London: S C M Press, 1974), pp. 45–50.
25 Above, pp. 39–40.
26 Alasdair MacIntyre, *Whose Justice? Which Rationality?* (London: Duckworth, 1988), p. 357.
27 Adrian Thatcher, 'Resurrection and Rationality' in P. Avis (ed.), *The Resurrection of Jesus Christ* (London: Marshall Pickering, 1990, forthcoming).

CHAPTER 7

Person, Nature and Man

What has been said about the divine subject in chapters 5 and 6 is of paramount importance for understanding what is perhaps the most contentious element of incarnational doctrine, viz. that Christ, the divine Person, had a human nature but lacked, or was not, a human person. Rather he became 'man', but the subject of his human nature, like that of his divine nature, was the divine Person of the Son. God the Son is a metaphysical Person whose divine nature becomes perfectly united to a human nature. There is one Person not two, and there are two natures, not one. In what senses, then, is Jesus a human person?

Jesus – a human person

In much catholic theology, surprisingly, Jesus Christ is not a human person at all. He is rather a man (*anthropos*, *homo*) whose human nature is perfectly united to his divine nature in the unity of the one (divine) Person. It is customary to speak of our Lord's 'manhood', which the Logos or divine Person assumes. According to Tertullian, 'person' seems to have meant 'an individuating quality which gives concrete reality to a general kind of being'.[1] Jesus, then, is generically a man. What makes the man Jesus God is the individuating quality of the Logos which gives concrete reality to his general, or generic, manhood. This doctrine is known by the strange phrase 'impersonal humanity'. His human person, then, in so far as it is proper to speak of his having one at all, lacks independent existence from God (it is *an-hypostatos*): he is human in nature only. The position is called *anhypostasia*, and is supported by the Chalcedonian definition, which states that 'the characteristic property of each nature' is preserved and concurs 'into one Person and one subsistence, not as if Christ were parted or divided into two persons, but one and the same Son and only-begotten God, Word, Lord, Jesus Christ . . .'. Less startling is the *enhypostatic* position, according to which Christ's humanity *is* concrete and hypostatic, but only inasmuch as and in so far as it subsists in the one divine Son.[2]

My purpose in raising the anhypostatic issue now is to demonstrate that the analogical method of approach to the Person of Christ adopted in these pages is fruitful even at this baffling and contentious impasse in Christology. Ordinary Christian believers are likely to be surprised to discover that according to catholic teaching Jesus Christ was not a human person, and doubly surprised at the intensity of disagreement which the issue continues to raise among contemporary writers. For some it is an 'astonishing doctrine', 'threatening the very core of his manhood', which must invite 'blank incomprehension in a modern listener'.[3] For others,[4] it is an essential truth of the faith which cannot admit compromise. Faced with such incompatible verdicts I shall again adopt a cautious position between conservation and commendation (discussed in chapter 1). The real divinity of Jesus is clearly at risk among the liberals, while the real humanity of Jesus is equally at risk among the conservatives. Perhaps the analogies so far developed can provide a way of protecting both.

Anthony Hanson holds 'that if you say Jesus was a complete human personality you cannot also hold the doctrine of hypostatic union (though I think there are many who hold both these beliefs in a confused way)'.[5] His impatience with the absence of a human person in Jesus is entirely justified, but is there really no way of holding both the real humanity and the real divinity of the one Christ? I shall now make two new proposals in order to provide a way out of this impasse. Both will need considerable justification. First, I shall preserve intact the metaphysical concept of Person as it is applied to the divine subject Jesus Christ, but regard modern uses of 'person' as equivalent to 'nature', i.e. to our Lord's human nature. His human nature will therefore be regarded as equivalent to his human personhood, and the list of (human) person concepts in chapter 1 will act as important qualifiers of his human nature. Second, I shall render the Chalcedonian definition's 'truly man' as 'truly a person'. There are several advantages to be gained from these proposals, but there are disadvantages too. Both must be discussed, and a case made out that the advantages outweigh the disadvantages. This will now be done. The divine Personhood and divine nature of Jesus are discussed further in chapter 8, where it is shown that these new proposals are consistent with the developing 'person/Person' analogy. A fuller account of 'truly a person, truly God' must be postponed until chapter 9.

When it is said by the Chalcedonian definition that Jesus is 'truly man', all that may be meant by 'man' is the generic term 'mankind' or 'humankind'. 'Truly man' need entail no more than that Jesus really did belong in some way to the human species. We have already seen that according to Thomas V. Morris Jesus did not need to be merely human in order to be fully human. Jean Galot and Eric Mascall, two more supporters of strict incarnational orthodoxy, insist that the human nature, while complete in itself, must be distinguished from the human subject whose nature it is.

And they reserve the term 'person' for the subject of the nature, which is divine.[6] In the human case, 'Person is defined as the *subject of consciousness and freedom*, but a distinction must be made between the subject who thinks and his intellect, the subject who wills and his will.'[7] In order to avoid the error that there are two subjects in the one Christ, the one divine Person 'is the subject of the human activities of consciousness and will. These activities in no sense imply that Jesus is a human person.'

The careful distinctions made in chapter 1 between different uses of the concept of the person will begin to clarify what the contemporary disagreement is about. These uses were classified as i) metaphysical, ii) philosophical, iii) psychological, iv) moral, v) existential, and vi) social. Part of the problem lies in a failure on both sides to appreciate the depth of the differences between the ancient use of i) and the more modern uses of ii)–vi). The Roman Catholic writer Edward Schillebeeckx is perhaps unusual among Catholics in allowing that Jesus may be called 'a human person', provided it is understood that to do so is to employ 'a humanly "secular" language-game'. In the language of faith, the *hypostasis* remains the divine Word.[8] Both Galot and Mascall allow that the human nature of Jesus is a dynamic entity, and 'the mentality of Jesus, like that of any other human being, developed *pari passu* with the development of his bodily organism'.[9] There seems little difficulty, then, in admitting Jesus to be a person in the psychological sense of having acquired a personality. 'Subject of consciousness and freedom' looks very like the existential concept of a person. What cause trouble are the largely undetected dissimilarities between the ancient and restricted concept of a person, where the person contributes to the individual's nature, and the modern inclusive concepts of the person, which encompass the individual's nature. This difference must now be spelled out.

Jesus – a divine Person only?

The root of the problem lies, I suspect, not in the ancient formulae themselves but in the attempt to force upon modern patterns of thinking about the person the ancient theological distinction between 'person' and 'nature'. Contemporary scholarship must obviously try to arrive at the plainest possible statement of the meanings of 'person' and 'nature' as they were affirmed by the ancient Church. But when this has been done it cannot overlook that contemporary thinking about the person draws on other sources which have caused 'person' and 'nature' to be much more broadly understood, with the result that a bold restatement of Chalcedonian orthodoxy may not be able to succeed merely by reintroducing into contemporary discourse how the relation between 'person' and 'nature' was once understood.

The words remain the same. The meanings do not.

I too want to defend Chalcedon, but I am not convinced that the best way of doing so is to situate its key terms in a different milieu where they are still expected to make good anthropological sense. Galot thinks much work in ontology still needs to be done on the distinction between person and nature. But I doubt whether this is a modern problem at all: it exercises only those whose concept of the person is fixed for all time by the ancient *hypostasis* and who believe they are somehow required to reinstate the ancient concepts of nature and person in modern philosophical anthropology just because of their undoubted centrality in traditional Christology. But it is one thing to inquire what Chalcedon means by 'Person' and 'nature' and quite another thing to offer a contemporary anthropology which purports to use the same pair of terms and the same contrasts between them in the same way. The use of 'nature' as a precise anthropological term is also fraught with problems.[10]

Another distinction crucial to Galot's incarnational orthodoxy is between being 'a man' and being 'a person'. One difference between the two is that 'Man experiences his own person in his social relationships and in his own psychological demeanor.'[11] A 'man' is the whole; 'person' and 'nature' are the parts. For Galot a 'man' is a duality of person and nature: he says the person alternately 'vivifies', or 'personifies' or 'personalizes' the nature.[12] Now if we can accept this anthropology as a contemporary way of thinking about ourselves, then we can agree that in the case of Jesus Christ the claim can intelligibly be made that it is the divine Person, not the human person, that 'vivifies' or animates the human nature. But if we cannot accept the anthropology, then we are unlikely to be able to accept the *anhypostasia* which depends on it.

Despite these criticisms of Galot, he claims for himself and for the Chalcedonian fathers a method which I have adopted here, viz. that of approaching the meaning of 'divine Person' through the meaning of 'human person'. With this I agree. But he goes on to claim that the fathers' use of *hypostasis* was 'based on the concrete notion of person as it emerges from the most commonplace human experience', 'an experience inseparably linked to the life of every human being and which, in its innermost reality, remains the same for everyone in every historical era and in every culture'.[13] This, I suggest, is simply false. People don't typically report their persons vivifying their natures, nor do they separate themselves from their persons and their natures in order to observe or describe what is going on. What Galot has rather obviously done is to have described the very general experience of being a human being in such a way that the ancient divisive concepts are written into it from the first. It is one particular description of human experience that Galot is interested in and generalizes from and one that carries little conviction today. There are of course no pre-suppositionless or concept-free descriptions of human experience, and my difficulty with Galot is not that he has failed to provide a sufficiently neutral account of human experience, but that he has offered as a plausible account of human individuality today one particular account of human experience which is constructed for a different purpose, viz. to support the *anhypostatic* doctrine.

Galot, then, stresses the individuality or particularity of the human person, something which the term *hypostasis* was designed to emphasize. My concepts ii)–v) also stress the individuality of the person (in this respect they probably owe something to the ancient concept), but they emphasize in their different ways what *kind* of individual the human being is, not how a human nature comes to be individuated or personalized. Indeed the idea of a general nature awaiting individuation is all too reminiscent of the *tabula rasa* concept of the mind passively waiting to be imprinted from without. The modern concepts also assume that developed personalness is the subject of wholeness and integration. They are inclusive concepts. If individuality is the main emphasis within the human being which the concept 'person' is employed to pick out, then at least it is easy to sympathize with the supporters of *anhypostasia*. They rightly protest that if Jesus is an internally centred, independent subsistence or person then he cannot simultaneously be the second Person of the Trinity. 'The heart of what they [the Chalcedonians] were denying is that he was a man apart from, independently of, God's indwelling of him'.[14]

But this sound traditionalist objection relies on a concept of a person which rests uneasily with contemporary descriptions of human being. Given the concept of a person which individuates a nature, to say that Jesus is both a divine Person and a human person is to affirm the absurdity (and heresy) of a duality of individuals within the one Christ. But there is an opposite danger, for when the doctrine that Jesus is a divine Person without also being a human person is brought alongside contemporary discussions of personhood, it appears to do violence to his complete solidarity with other people and to portray his real humanity as deficient. Galot is of course keenly aware of the difficulty, yet despite strenuous efforts he fails to avoid it. If he is to avoid a deficient account of our Lord's real humanity he must show that the entire lack of a human person in the divine Christ is consistent with his real and complete humanness.

His attempt to save the real humanity of Christ from deficiency proceeds by drawing a further distinction of his own between a concept of the human person which is 'the totality of the human being' (Strawson's concept of the person would be a good example), and a more restricted concept of a person where what the person is only contributes to the nature. This contribution, he says, is in the case of Jesus Christ provided by the divine Word.[15] But he still cannot explain at all why, given that Christ has no human person to contribute to his nature, he is not deficient as a human being. Galot commits himself to person/nature distinctions which have their time-honoured place in ancient anthropology. But the price he pays for using them is heavy. They do not hook up with modern discussions of the person, and the descriptions of our Lord's real humanity which 'in no sense imply that Jesus is a human person' invite disbelief. This is a point which must be made with some force. Galot has already made the distinction, in the case of the human person, between 'the subject who thinks and his intellect, the subject who wills and his will'. This subject *is* the human person. In Christ the subject is the divine Person. The absence of a human subject in Jesus Christ is plainly impossible to reconcile with his real humanity. Ironically, an alternative approach is suggested by Galot's own analysis. If he had persevered with the person concept which he himself acknowledges as 'the totality of the human being', the missing link between ancient and modern anthropology might have been installed.

Two more defenders of orthodoxy

I conclude that the employment of this restricted and exclusive concept of a human person alongside more recent inclusive concepts can hardly fail to mislead inquirers into the Christian faith by compromising our Lord's real humanity. The point will now be emphasized further by showing how two recent defenders of orthodoxy, Thomas V. Morris and Brian Hebblethwaite, produce (although to differing degrees) a similar unfortunate effect. Morris, describing why Aquinas refused to acknowledge the human personhood of Jesus, shows how Aquinas suggests that the terms 'person', '*hypostasis*' and '*suppositum*' (i.e. a bearer of properties) refer to 'a whole of a certain kind'. 'The implication', says Morris, 'is that nothing, in so far as it is a part rather than a whole, qualifies as a *suppositum*, *hypostasis*, or person.'[16] Now 'a man' is clearly a whole of parts, and so must clearly qualify as a person or *hypostasis*. But the man Jesus does not so qualify, for

> the case of Christ is unique. In Christ the human body and soul were not an independent whole, but were joined to the divine person of God the Son, as the human nature in which the divine *suppositum* dwelt. Not being an independent whole, but only a part of that greater whole which was God Incarnate, they did not alone constitute a person or characterize a *suppositum* dwelling in both divine and human natures.[17]

Armed with his crucial distinction between mere humanity and real humanity, Morris concedes that while it may be impossible for mere humans to have only one mind, Jesus possessed two minds, a divine mind and a human mind. His human mind together with his body are parts of that single whole which, with the divine nature, is the divine Person of the Son.

Again orthodoxy is preserved, but at too great a cost. Mere humans are persons; God the Son is a divine Person only. God the Son has subsumed a real humanity, though, as we have seen in chapter 4, the new contrast between real humanity and mere humanity actually serves to obscure the real humanhood of Jesus (*formal* humanity would be a more precise designation). What is especially interesting about Morris's use of Aquinas's argument is that the unfortunate contrast between real and mere humanity is invoked in support of it. But for Aquinas (and of course for orthodoxy) Jesus has a human nature, and this is certainly a *suppositum*, for 'a nature is something like a set of properties any instance of the joint instantiation of which we consider an individual of that nature'.[18] And the human nature or *suppositum* which is exemplified by Jesus is presumably a whole in its exemplification.

Part of the trouble here is the difficulty of describing how parts are related to wholes. Some parts of wholes are themselves wholes. More will be made of this distinction in chapter 9. But the new problem for orthodoxy now is that the price of its defence is the depiction of Jesus as one whose humanity is actually incomplete. Although his humanity is said to be 'real' and 'complete', it becomes more limited than our own. Jesus cannot be constituted as a human individual without the divine Person which alone individuates him. Now in addition to real humanity and mere humanity there is complete humanity and incomplete humanity. I doubt whether ordinary Christians could accept the incomplete humanity of Jesus, but that is exactly what orthodoxy unpacked in this way requires them to do. The human Jesus, who on this view is no human person, requires his divinity to constitute his humanity. The doctrine has the astounding consequence for pastoral theology that Jesus is not a whole human person.

Hebblethwaite's position is closer to the one which is developing in this work.[19] The doctrines of *anhypostasia* and *enhypostasia*, he says,

> must not be taken to imply that Jesus lacked a human mind, will, consciousness or personality. But they do imply that the metaphysical subject of the human life of Jesus was the eternal Son of God, and that we cannot think of the man Jesus apart from his being God incarnate.[20]

The question to be faced is whether this position is consistent. Jesus, then, has a human personality. God, Hebblethwaite says, came among us 'as a particular man'. 'God comes face to face with us as another human being'.[21] He speaks of 'the real humanity of

Jesus', of 'the man Jesus',[22] and of 'the human subject, Jesus'.[23] 'Jesus was certainly a member of the species *homo sapiens*,' 'a real man with a particular history and social context behind and around him'.[24] Can Jesus be what Hebblethwaite rightly says he is, yet not be a human person too?

This is not just Hebblethwaite's problem; it is a problem for orthodoxy. It is hard to see how Jesus could have had a human personality without also being a human person. When people read that Jesus is a real man, or a human subject, or a member of the human species, are they not entitled to assume, with the vast majority of Christians, that the words (for once) have a straightforward non-technical sense, not a restricted technical sense? Jesus was and is one of us, and it was and is as one of us that God came among us and suffered and died. I think Hebblethwaite struggles valiantly with this problem. He says the metaphysical subject of the human life of Jesus was the eternal Son of God. Elsewhere he says 'The primary subject of all christological statements is God . . . We are not talking of two separate individuals, but of the divine substance, which is such as to include within its own subjectivity the human subject, Jesus, as the expression and vehicle of God's incarnate life.'[25] The interesting question to raise is whether, in speaking of a metaphysical subject, Hebblethwaite would also allow a non-metaphysical, i.e. a *human*, subject; and whether in speaking of a primary subject, he would be prepared to allow a *secondary* subject, viz. the human being Jesus.

Jesus, 'truly a person'

The doctrine of our Lord's impersonal humanity is in danger of jeopardizing the real and particular humanness of Jesus. As we have seen, it can deny human subjectness in Christ, and it can produce a deficient and incomplete humanity. One advantage of speaking of Jesus as 'fully a person' is that it emphasizes clearly in a modern context his total solidarity with all other men and women, 'like us in all things apart from sin'. A second advantage is that a direct link is established between the theological tradition and the strong interest expressed in the human person at the present time. More recent accounts of persons now become unambiguously applicable to the human nature of Jesus Christ. Third, I claim, despite certain opposition, that to ascribe to Jesus human personhood is consistent with a developing orthodoxy. When in the fourth century the terms 'person', 'nature' and 'man' were applied to Jesus Christ the Church was not committed in advance to static theories about the meaning of each; indeed, as Bernard Lonergan has remarked, when the Chalcedonian fathers used the terms 'person' and 'nature' to express the truth of God, the concepts were 'heuristic', i.e. they were deliberately chosen so as to be open to further interpretation, but contained just enough content to 'iden-tify the objects to which they are applied'.[26] It is at least arguable that to be a human person and to have a human nature are con-gruous to a degree not previously thought possible. But, as I shall shortly suggest, it is a mistake to treat 'nature' too prescriptively, so only a little weight is being placed on this suggestion.

The same advantages work for rendering 'truly man' as 'truly a person'. That Jesus is 'truly man' affirms his 'belongingness' to the species 'man'. That much seems to be agreed by everyone. What cannot be agreed is whether Jesus in being 'like us in all things apart from sin' may also and for that reason be called 'truly a person'. My case for 'truly a person' (the meaning of the phrase is developed further in chapter 9) rests simply on two factors. First, a being who is not a human person cannot enjoy solidarity with beings who are human beings. Second, an alternative way of ex-pressing the orthodox position suggests itself, and that is what is being attempted in this book.

What, then, are the disadvantages of 'truly a person, truly a God'? It may be held to be discontinuous with the Christian tradi-tion. I think this charge is unfair, for the concept of a person is so much more extensively used now than it was in the first five cen-turies of Christianity that the real humanity of Jesus is hard to express without it. Careful distinctions have been made between the metaphysical concept and the remaining concepts, so there is no danger of elision from one to the other. The old error of positing two persons within the one Christ is avoided for the same reason. 'Person' and 'person' have markedly distinct uses, some of which overlap. The strongest disadvantage is that 'Person', as applied to Christ in the tradition, unites the divine and human natures, whereas 'truly a person, truly God', might be thought to destroy the unity between God and humankind which 'Person' provides: 'person' gets unwarrantably confined to the human side only in the phrase 'truly a person, truly God'. My answer to the difficulty is that there are two types of person-concept involved, the ancient metaphysical concept of Person and the modern concepts of the human person represented by ii)–vi) early in the chapter (and in-troduced in chapter 1). The analogy emphasizes and preserves the unity of the divine and human natures in the one divine Person of Christ. The analogy includes the human person Jesus of Nazareth in the divine Person of the Son while emphasizing equally the single Personhood of God the Son, the perfect personhood of Jesus of Nazareth, and their unity. More work has yet to be done on the identity of the divine/human subject, and this is attempted in chap-ter 8.

The two natures of Christ

The ontology of the creeds is there to guide and not simply to constrain. The ancient faith may be better commended by the revision of some of its ontological categories. Does 'nature' need to be revised as well? Morris uses 'nature' with great precision. The divine and human natures of Jesus are understood as 'natural-kind terms', and 'According to one standard account of natural kinds, every such kind has an essence, a set of properties or underlying traits individually necessary and jointly sufficient for membership in the kind.'[27] The human and divine natures of Jesus may be understood in this way, with the result that Jesus may be understood as possessing those sets of properties which make him fully (but not merely) human, and fully divine. But as we have seen the two-natures tradition need not itself be taken as part of a successful defence of orthodoxy.[28] One wonders, following Lonergan's suggestion, whether the doctrine of our Lord's two natures should not be too concisely defined, precisely in order to allow for further development and for religious sensitivity to the divine mystery it protects. Clarity, however desirable, is sometimes not enough. Any account of what is meant by 'nature', including Morris's, cannot help but be stipulative, but it should not be overprescriptive. And, following the work of Ryle and Wittgenstein already discussed in chapter 5, it is a simple matter to add 'nature' to the list of terms which are disastrously prone to category mistakes. The ossified term 'nature' as applied to Christ can easily suggest 'thinghood'. One time-honoured way of stating who Jesus is is to say he is a divine Person in two natures. The ascription of two natures is intended as an aid to our recognition of the mystery of his being, not as a source of some further information about him which makes the recognition more difficult. Christology for today must be based on the two-nature orthodoxy, but I do not think it should be required to retain the term 'nature' as an explanatory category unless of course it is useful to do so.

The position advocated here is close to that advocated by Brian Davies in his *Thinking about God*. He suggests that 'To ascribe a nature to something is to say what the thing is, and this, in turn, is *to locate the thing linguistically*.'[29] Here we may again notice the shift from reference to use, common in recent philosophy of language:

> Recognizing that something is a such and such (a human being or a snowdrop) is having some grasp of how the thing can intelligibly be talked about. As when we say that something is a person, when we say that something has such and such a nature we are not so much describing as indicating how we should speak.

This remark about the meaning of our talk about natures reproduces what has already been claimed for some of our talk about
persons, where what appeared to be descriptions turned out on
examination to be 'indications' or, at any rate, indirectly referring
statements with unstraightforward referents. So, continues Davies,

> What, then, of 'Christ had two natures, divine and human'? What does
> that mean? Given that we can say 'Christ is a person', at least part of the
> answer is surely obvious. To say that Christ had a human nature and a
> divine nature is to say that Christ was a subject of whom we can talk in
> two different ways. It is to say that with Christ it is true to say of him
> what it is appropriate to say both of what is human and of what is
> divine.[30]

The line of argument pursued in this book supports Davies's position. The development of complementarity in chapter 4, together
with the ontological reasons for doing so, makes easier the recognition of Christ as 'a subject of whom we can talk in two different
ways'. Traditional talk about his two natures states claims about
the legitimacy of ascribing both Godhood and humanhood to him.
'So the main point is that if we say that Christ is one person with a
human nature and a divine nature, we are licensing statements like
"Christ was tired" and "Christ was omnipotent".'[31] Whether
'omnipotence' should be included among the properties which it is
appropriate to ascribe to Jesus Christ during the limitations of his
earthly life is discussed in the next chapter. Here the term at least
provides a clear example of the sort of claims that belong to one
particular way of talking about him (reminiscent of our
D-predicates).

I hope by now to have shown that the pursuit of the basic person
analogy, thus far at least, has not led to theological improprieties
and may even have provided a fresh approach towards the ontological issues which the doctrine of the incarnation raises. Our
Lord's divine nature is discussed in the next chapter, where a new
person analogy is introduced. I take his possession of two natures
to mean that while he was a human person he was also fully God,
and that he who was fully God became fully a human person. In
other words he was a person who was both human and divine, and
in this sense of 'person' upper and lower case are equally appropriate. He was, and is, God in person, and this is a claim which may or
may not be stated for today by recourse to the term 'nature'.

Reluctantly I conclude that strict adherence to the actual terms
used at Chalcedon undermines the attempt to commend convincingly the real humanity of Jesus to an age where 'person' and to a
lesser extent 'nature' have acquired new and bewilderingly different meanings. In any case, the fathers at Chalcedon were doubtless conscious of ambiguities in the language they used, and might
never have come to an agreement at all if their terms had been too

precisely defined. None the less Chalcedon remains the most adequate historical expression of Christology available to the Church
and it is still able to inspire alternative approaches to our limited
grasp of God's being in Christ.

The analogical approach: the middle way

Let us now take stock and see whether the anhypostatic impasse, if
not solvable, is avoidable. Here our analogical approach to the
Person of Christ may be of assistance. It began with the assumption, derived from Irenaeus and embodied in the Chalcedonian
definition, that Jesus is truly God and truly man. Next a clear
analogical basis was found to exist for comparing the human person with the divine Person. There is good patristic warrant for this,
and we have noted that both the development of Logos-
Christology and the employment of the concept *hypostasis* from the
fourth century onwards represent parallel ways of beginning theological work with the experience of being a person, and then refin-
ing the conceptual content of that experience before applying it to
God. Use was then made of a modern concept of a person, and a
series of striking structural parallels as built which suggested that a
modern double-aspect account of the person might provide many
gains for Christian orthodoxy: gains both in providing an account
of the human being which avoids Platonic and Cartesian dualism
at a time when dualism is very properly questioned; and, more
importantly, in providing a different pattern for modelling the divine Person on the human person. The 'person theory' then set the
scene for a different kind of theological exploration.

When the exploration was continued it was discovered that
being a person did not merely legitimize the use of complementary
languages (strictly defined): it made them necessary. So it came as
no surprise to discover that the Chalcedonian definition was itself
an obvious example of complementarity, for here too an account of
a Person was being attempted. The subject of the account was
transcendent, and not just by virtue of being a person: his transcendence was really divine. Further exploration yielded the result that
a person is to be accorded the status of a primary substance provided it was not characterized by 'thinghood'. Each of us is a
person, yet the explication of personhood transcends objective description, allowing real indirect reference by means of our language
to our personal states. God's Word, Wisdom and Spirit were seen
analogously to be forms of personal language providing real though
indirect reference to the states of God's very being. The transcendence of the human person over the human understanding of the
person further assisted the analogy by suggesting how the divine
Person might also transcend human formulations of it.

In chapter 6 we observed that in the human person who takes on his own lips the revelatory name of God and uses the human power of self-ascription to avow his Godhood, the elusive personal God becomes finally revealed. The 'I' of the 'I am' sayings may, despite honest historical difficulties, be the divine embodied 'I' which permanently refashions the human understanding of God, but it is also a human 'I' which speaks. The human nature of Jesus is not 'dominated' or 'possessed' by the divine Person, as Galot says;[32] rathèr his human life is so at one with the life of God that it becomes appropriate to say it was 'one in being' with it.

This chapter leaves open the possibility that, confronted with an orthodoxy which denies the reality of the human person of Christ in order to give due prominence to the divine Person of the Son, an alternative expression of orthodoxy may have suggested itself which may be able to commend the orthodox teaching while conserving the meaning, if not the actual traditional terms, of the faith. It begins by affirming the human person of Jesus and then proceeds by a series of analogies to affirm the identity of God the Son with him. There is a single divine/human 'I' which is the subject of both our Lord's natures. The formulation 'one Person in two natures' could also be rendered as 'a subject of whom we can talk in two different ways'. The 'two person' error is avoided by drawing attention to the differences between the ancient and modern concepts of the person. We no longer speak of men and women as beings whose natures are animated by their persons. The divine and human subjects are appropriately located within each of the two complementary languages. We saw that a reason for denying the human person of Jesus was that the divine Person could not unite himself with an 'internally centred, independent subsistence'. But perhaps the independence of Jesus as a human being does not after all subvert his unity with God the Son, for his sinlessness may enable him to be independent without being separate. Other analogies, also drawn from the human person, may yet help us here, and they are considered in chapters 8 and 9.

NOTES

1   See A. Richardson and J. Bowden (eds), *A New Dictionary of Christian Theology* (London: SCM Press, 1983), p. 443.

2   John of Damascus, *Dialectica*, 44. See Richardson and Bowden (eds), *A New Dictionary of Christian Theology*, p. 44.

3   J. A. T. Robinson, *The Human Face of God* (London: SCM Press, 1973), pp. 105, 106, 39. Anthony Hanson, after a thorough survey of contemporary Christology, also rejects it. See his *The Image of the Invisible God* (London: SCM Press, 1982), ch. 1. The work is an attempt to provide a conservative alternative to anhypostatic orthodoxy.

4   Karl Barth, Emil Brunner, Eric Mascall, Thomas Torrance, Jean Galot and Graham Leonard all support it.

5   Hanson, *The Image of the Invisible God*, p. 23. I suspect he may think I too am confused.

6   Jean Galot SJ, *Who is Christ? A Theology of the Incarnation* (Rome: Gregorian University Press, 1980); Eric Mascall, 'On From Chalcedon' in *Whatever Happened to the Human Mind?* (London: SPCK, 1980), p. 35. Mascall has an admiring summary of Galot's earlier work in Christology in his *Theology and the Gospel of Christ* (London: SPCK, 1977), ch. 3.

7   Galot, *Who is Christ?*, p. 284.

8   Edward Schillebeeckx, *Jesus* (London: Collins Fount, 1983), pp. 657–8. Schillebeeckx was closely questioned about his use of the expression 'human person' in connection with Christ, and quickly reverted to a more orthodox statement of his position. See Peter Hebblethwaite, *The New Inquisition?* (London: Collins Fount, 1980), pp. 143–4.

9   Mascall, *Whatever Happened to the Human Mind?*, p. 44: Galot, *Who is Christ?*, p. 285.

10 John Stuart Mill's hard-headed analysis of 'nature' indicates the level of difficulty involved. See his essay 'Nature' in *Three Essays on Religion*, 1850–74, *Collected Works of John Stuart Mill*. vol. 10 (University of Toronto Press: Routledge and Kegan Paul, 1969), pp. 373–402.

11 Galot, *Who is Christ?*, p. 281.

12 ibid., pp. 285, 286, 300.

13 ibid., pp. 280–1.

14 Robinson, *The Human Face of God*, p. 41.

15 Galot, *Who is Christ?*, p. 293.

16 Thomas V. Morris, *The Logic of God Incarnate* (Ithaca and London: Cornell University Press, 1986), p. 156.

17 ibid., p. 157.

18 ibid., p. 155.

19 Ever since the publication of *The Myth of God Incarnate*, Brian Hebblethwaite has maintained a spirited defence of a more orthodox position in a series of essays and articles. These are now available in the collection entitled *The Incarnation* (Cambridge: Cambridge University Press, 1987). My position is often close to his.

20 ibid., p. 70.

21 ibid., pp. 1, 4.

22 ibid., p. 22.

23 ibid., p. 31.

24 ibid., p. 158.

25 ibid., p. 31. See also p. 164.

26 Bernard Lonergan, *A Second Collection* (London: Darton, Longman & Todd, 1974), p. 259.

27 Morris, *The Logic of God Incarnate*, p. 22.

28 above. p. 83.

29 Brian Davies, *Thinking About God* (London: Geoffrey Chapman, 1985), p. 290, emphasis added. It is worth noting that the book is one in a series called 'Introducing Catholic Theology', and by receipt of the *nihil obstat* and *imprimatur* is considered to be free from doctrinal error.

30 ibid., p. 291.

31 ibid.

32 Galot, *Who is Christ?*, p. 300: hardly the languge of mutuality and filiality!

CHAPTER 8

Persons and Anomalies

An argument was developed in the previous chapter for the conclusion that the human nature of Jesus could stand as an equivalent for his human personhood. How is this position consistent with his possession of a divine nature, and with his being one? What account might be given of his divine nature? The present chapter opens with two contrasting approaches to the omnipotence of the incarnate Christ. Since he is truly God and is therefore endowed with a divine nature, he is expected by some to possess undiminished omnipotence throughout his earthly life. Others see his powerlessness as the clue to his divinity. An impasse between these two approaches provides the context for a new person analogy which has yet to feature in the series. It is based on the theory of 'anomalous monism'. The theory will be outlined, and I shall argue that this account of the human person, with its particular emphases on mystery and transcendence, provides novel but fruitful analogues into the mysterious divine nature of the incarnate Christ. As in previous chapters, the analogical approach to the Person of Christ provides a middle way between contrasting conservative and liberal approaches.

Did the incarnate Christ have two minds?

According to the traditional view defended by Morris, Jesus Christ maintained every attribute of deity without diminution or change, before, during and after his incarnate life. The doctrine of kenosis, that the incarnate Son voluntarily laid aside some of, or some measure of, his divine attributes throughout his incarnate life, is rejected.[1] The incarnate Christ is said to have had two minds, corresponding to the two natures.[2] The divine mind had access to the human mind, but the human mind only had that access to the divine mind that the divine mind allowed it to have. This 'double-minded' view of Jesus is claimed to be superior to kenotic views, for 'It is not by virtue of what he gave up, but in virtue of what he took on, that he humbled himself.'[3] With regard to his temptations, there are at least two reasons why Jesus, being fully God, could not do evil. The first is that anyone who sins or does evil must have the property of 'being such that one possibly sins'. But this property is a property of being only merely human; it does not belong to being 'fully human'.[4] Since Jesus was fully human, but not merely human, he lacked the property of being such that he could possibly sin. Second, in choosing good 'it must be admitted from the outset that he could not have chosen otherwise. His divine nature would have prevented it.'[5]

This position is unsatisfactory. Once more the dubious distinction between full humanity and mere humanity is employed in order to isolate Jesus from large sectors of (merely) human experience.[6] Indeed Jesus finally ends up with no human mind at all, for

> He was not a being endowed with a set of personal cognitive and casual powers distinct from the cognitive and causal powers of God the Son. For Jesus was the same person as God the Son. Thus, the personal cognitive and causal powers operative in the case of Jesus' earthly mind were just none other than the cognitive and causal powers of God the Son. The results of their operation through the human body . . . were just such as to give rise to a human mind . . . [7]

The human mind of Jesus is, then, just the divine mind operating under the limitations of an earthly body. In effect the human mind is a pseudonym for the divine mind operating under earthly conditions. Here surely is a fine example of Apollinarianism masquerading as a tight defence of orthodoxy. And there are many other problems as well. Since being able to sin is a property of being only 'merely human', and since not being able to sin is a property of being 'fully human', we may speculate that being 'fully human' is possible only for an individual whose 'personal cognitive and causal powers are the personal cognitive and causal powers of God himself'. That is, to be fully human *is* to be divine. As the divinity of Jesus is increasingly emphasized, so is his humanity diminished, and his solidarity with 'mere humans' becomes a charade. The picture of a double-minded Person merely reinforces the impression gained as Morris's argument gathers pace that Jesus' 'real humanity' is a remote essence of little interest or relevance to anyone, especially anyone who hopes to discover in Jesus God's gracious coming among us as one of us, not just as an exemplification in a formal essence.

Was the incarnate Christ omnipotent?

Let us now consider a starkly contrasting approach to the omnipotence of Jesus, provided by Dietrich Bonhoeffer's lectures on Christology in 1933. These are his reported words:

> If we speak of Jesus Christ as God, we may not speak of him as the representative of an idea of God who possesses the properties of omniscience and omnipotence (there is no such thing as this abstract divine nature!); we must speak of his weakness, of the cradle and the cross; and this man is no abstract God.[8]

Again, Christian thought is polarized. According to the former view the affirmation of the divine nature of Jesus also requires that he possessed all the attributes of deity during his incarnate life, including of course omnipotence. According to the latter view, his powerlessness is the surest sign of his Godhood. The analogy soon to be developed will chart a middle way through these polarities. But let us first allow omnipotence to stand as an example of the divine attributes which, given Jesus' divine nature, he might be thought to possess, and ask how essential omnipotence is to belief in the divine nature.

Much philosophical discussion about divine omnipotence is about the formidable logical problems involved. There is disagreement about whether God's alleged omnipotence can ever be satisfactorily formulated,[9] and even those who think it can disagree about the result.[10] Can an omnipotent God control free human beings?[11] There is also disagreement among theologians whether omnipotence ought to be regarded as an attribute of God at all.[12] With regard to the Christological problem of the omnipotence of God the Son, there is further disagreement between those who affirm the 'classical' and the 'kenotic' positions,[13] or variant versions of each.

One solution, toyed with by Morris, requires further qualification of the divine attributes in the light of the incarnation, so that whatever God has power to do or know must be qualified by the kenotic limitations imposed by the incarnation.[14] Another solution emphasizes the difference between philosophical reflection on God's attributes and theological reflection on God's revealed nature.[15] Here the neo-orthodox theologian Emil Brunner (whose hostility to philosophy does not vitiate his fine theological insights) contrasts a speculative concept of omnipotence, a *potestas absoluta* or *omnipotentia*, with the revelation of the biblical God who has power 'over all'. 'Revelation . . . teaches nothing about *omnipotentia*. The biblical concept means God's power over the whole universe.' God, continues Brunner, is 'Free and Sovereign Lord, whose power cannot be limited by anything or anyone.' The decisive difference between the biblical and the speculative understanding of omnipotence is 'the self-limitation of God through and for His creation. Here, in the Cross of Christ, where the decisive saving Act takes place, this self-limitation reaches its climax . . .'[16]

Brunner's handling of omnipotence is similar to my earlier remarks about the incarnation causing an upheaval in the categories customarily employed in talk about God.[17] Faced with a real revelation of God in Christ, prior categories like divinity and humanity struggle to accommodate what is believed to have taken place through the incarnation. The incarnation causes a similar upheaval in our language about the divine attributes. The traditional attributes of God are the product of important philosophical reflection, much of it *a priori*, on what God must be, simply in order to be God. But suppose one engages instead in a parallel theological reflection on what God reveals of himself through the death and resurrection of Christ and the coming of the Spirit. This kind of reflection led the author of 1 John to conclude that 'God is love' (1 John 4.8,16). What must the attributes of God be in order for him to reveal himself as the triune God whom Christians worship? As the process theologians often say, a lover who can elicit a free response from the beloved has more power over him or her than one who by coercion can compel involuntary assent,[18] with the result that talk about what it is logically possible for God to be able to do gets overtaken by a different topic of religious importance, viz. the operation of God's saving love.

Did the incarnate Christ have two wills?

Must Christians be committed to the view that the divine nature of Jesus was, or contained, a separate centre of consciousness? We have already had reason to discount this suggestion.[19] Intention, agency and consciousness are of course ascribed by Christians to God, but it is the Godhead which is normally the subject of the ascriptions. God has a divine consciousness appropriate to being God; Jesus has a human consciousness appropriate to being a person. Does Jesus have one consciousness or two? The question is similar to another, viz. 'Did Jesus have one will or two?' The view that he had a single will was condemned by the third Council of Constantinople in 680. The orthodox position excludes two rival positions. It excludes the single-will, or 'monothelite', position, and in so doing it safeguards the human will of Jesus. The divine will is not allowed so to supervene upon the human will that in effect there is only a single will. And it also excludes the position that Jesus has a human will only. Hebblethwaite reminds us that 'incarnational Christology attributes two consciousnesses, not to Jesus, but to God incarnate'.[20] But he is understandably reticent about their relation. He allows that 'the human expression of divine attributes requires self-limitation in a way in which the divine awareness of the human experience does not'.[21] On this view there remain two consciousnesses, but the possibility of the divine consciousness becoming limited in its incarnate form is allowed for.

The reasons for affirming two wills in the one Chirst belong to seventh-century controversy and cannot be allowed to detain us. We might note that the Council of Constantinople seems to have assigned a will to each of the two natures of Christ, but since wills are assignable to persons rather than to natures, the doctrine of two wills runs into philosophical and psychological difficulties.[22] The position being adopted in this essay could be made consistent with a modified version of the two wills or 'dyothelite' doctrine. It is possible to urge that talk of each will belongs to the complementary languages which the one Person of Christ makes necessary, and, since an argument was mounted in the last chapter supporting the human personhood of Christ, it would be possible to reassign a will to each. There is, however, a fairly obvious danger in doing so. It appears to make little psychological sense to talk of a person with two wills. Also, the work already undertaken on person language in chapter 5 should make us wary of treating 'wills' as assignable 'things' at all. The analogy about to be developed in the present chapter may provide an alternative way forward. I return to this topic at the end of this chapter.

We have again reached a familiar impasse. Liberal Christology is in the main content with a human Jesus who is a uniquely inspired man. Conservative Christology ends up with a double consciousness and a dubiously real humanity. Against the liberals we might want to insist that, if Jesus is only a man uniquely inspired by God, then the complete solidarity of God the Son with humankind is lost. Again, if the sufferings of Jesus were not the sufferings of God, then God does not take upon himself human pain and dereliction; and if the vulnerability of Jesus to human wickedness is not also the vulnerability of God's own self-giving, then it is not God's love that is disclosed in Christ's cross. For these and other reasons the Godhood of Jesus must be insisted on. On the other hand there are at least two types of conservatism which, in insisting on the Godhood of Jesus, weaken his humanity. First, the conservative philosophical theology of Morris is controlled by modal concepts of God which are too far removed from revelation. Second, the conservative evangelicals have in the main shied away from the religious implications of a real humanity which embraces real temptations, doubts, fears, and so on. The analogical approach which I shall now attempt to unfold again offers a middle way through the disputed territory.

A new analogy: anomalous monism

The analogy chosen in this present chapter is based on a recent person theory called 'anomalous monism'. Anomalous monism is a theory which indicates that we are ourselves baffling mysteries with respect to our conscious states, mysteries which bring about the breakdown of talk about their causes, and so on. Given that there is unfathomability and mystery in the human case, we may well expect to find replication and intensification of both in the divine case of the Person of Christ. The philosophical difficulties encountered in positing the free human subject are importantly like the theological difficulties encountered in positing the divine/human subject Jesus Christ. In each case language struggles with the ontological depth it attempts to convey. Like the person theory in chapter 2 anomalous monism may be unfamiliar to theological readers whose patience is again sought throughout the short philosophical description which follows. The eventual implications for Christology are far-reaching.

Anomalous monism is the name given to a recent philosophical attempt to account for the presence of mental or psychological events in a physical world. It is monistic with regard to the person, because it accepts that a person is a single entity. Yet instead of identifying mental states with physical states, as a monistic theory might be expected to do, it accepts that mental states are literally anomalous with respect to material laws. Anomalous monism is a refined materialism in that its supporters hold that 'psychological events are describable, taken one by one, in physical terms, that is, they are physical events'.[23] It is called 'monism' because 'it holds that psychological events are physical events'; and it is 'anomalous' because 'it insists that events do not fall under strict laws when described in psychological terms.' The theory 'resembles materialism in its claim that all events are physical, but rejects the thesis, usually considered essential to materialism, that mental phenomena can be given purely physical explanations'. So what already emerges as a novel development is that the theory sides with materialism, and so against dualism, while firmly repudiating the tendency of materialism to adopt reductive descriptions of mental events.

Donald Davidson, the main proponent of the theory, explains the centrality of the anomalous element as follows:

> We explain a man's free actions, for example, by appeal to his desires, habits, knowledge and perceptions. Such accounts of intentional behavior operate in a conceptual framework removed from the direct reach of physical law by describing both cause and effect, reason and action, as aspects of a portrait of a human agent. The anomalism of the mental is thus a necessary condition for viewing action as autonomous.[24]

Without moral freedom, then, there can be no moral agency, yet an account of moral freedom is something which materialism simply cannot be expected to provide. We are back with something like the position of Abelson in chapter 5. Abelson identified two basic types of descriptions which belong to human action. Physical descriptions involve the use of terms such as object, event, cause, neuron, and so on; psychological descriptions involve the use of terms such as reason, intention, action, choice, and so on.

According to Davidson anomalous monism relies on three premises. First, 'psychological events such as perceivings, rememberings, the acquisition and loss of knowledge, and intentional actions are directly or indirectly caused by, and the causes of physical events.' Second, 'when events are related as cause and effect, then there exists a closed and deterministic system of laws into which these events, when appropriately described, fit'. However, third, 'there are no precise psycho-physical laws'.[25] That there can be no such laws is established by a simple consideration of a person's explanation of why he or she acts in a certain way. This is because an explanation of an action will involve a wider reference to overall beliefs, goals, intentions or attributions of meaning, and laws clearly cannot be formulated to cover all these. In any case the psychical side of individuals may be too complex *ever* to be stated as following general laws. For if reasons for acting are causes of actions, then, so the argument runs, there must be *some* laws in operation, even if we do not know what they are, because to claim that one event is the cause of another is to claim that some sort of causal law is in operation.

The example of an ex-smoker who quits because he believes it damages his health will illustrate the three premises. By premise i) the action of refraining from smoking can be said to be caused in part by the psychological state of believing that smoking is harmful. Yet by premise ii) no one can say how the belief was instrumental in bringing about the effect. Now to understand an action as performed because reasons for it have been given is to say that reasons belong somewhere in the causal story. But by premise ii) to say one thing is the cause of another is to say that a system of cause and effect is in operation, even though by premise iii) we cannot fill out the details of how the belief brings about the effect. This is because beliefs and other psychological states like desires and dispositions are not the sort of things that can be subsumed under physical laws; and it is also because psychological states are inextricably related to the biographies of their subjects, so that precise scientific laws governing an almost infinite number of psychological states of persons may be contingently impossible.

Davidson's second premise leads him to a materialism where one is not obliged to follow. It should be noted, none the less, that here is a version of materialism which preserves the freedom of the individual against determinism and stresses the unpredictability of human action when subjected to scientific description. The utter, disastrous failure of social science to predict human action has been well stated by MacIntyre.[26] Anomalous monism is unlike Strawson's theory in that it allows that persons are wholly material beings whose actions are anomalous with a material world. Strawson's theory makes the person a mysterious entity to whom both mental and physical predicates are equally applicable. None the less the theories are reconcilable. According to the person theory a person is a material object together with that to which P-predicates are ascribable; according to anomalous monism a person is a material object together with whatever makes psychological events anomalous. But no attempt has to be made to show the compatibility between the two theories. Anomalous monism is brought alongside the person theory because it may provide additional insights which can be applied to that mystery which is the Person of Christ.

A final advantage of anomalous monism is its confession of ignorance about the nature of mental and emotional states. 'Anomalous' suggests an unfathomability about the facts of human consciousness, for to be able to act freely is already to presuppose a level of being which can transcend predictability, and which defies the cold application of causal laws. The theory even gives rise to Bernard Williams's suggestion that philosophy may be mistaken about the possibility of approaching the facts of consciousness *at all*, because 'the *only* perspective on the contents of A's consciousness is the perspective of A's consciousness'.[27] The distinction we have already drawn between first-person perspectives and third-person perspectives[28] underlines the radical contribution Williams here makes to the philosophy of mind. Third-person observations and first-person descriptions of the contents of consciousness cannot be reconciled, he says, because 'there can be no third-personal perspective on the contents of consciousness'. On this view a purely physicalist account of consciousness undoubtedly leaves problems, but these arise from the incorrigible character of a person's conscious states, which defies proper expression and exposes the weaknesses in *any* conceptual scheme which tries to account for them. Williams seems to admit to a resigned scepticism about the power of human thought to include itself in any account of the human person which is, at the same time, the product of thought:

> Many of the most immediate and seemingly overwhelming objections to physicalism stem from the thought that there is no way to incorporate into the physicalist picture of things the existence of the contents of consciousness. There is not, but that is no objection, if there is no coherent way of regarding the contents of consciousness from an objective or third-personal point of view at all.

I think anomalous monism turns out to be not an explanation of human action, but a stylish confession of the absence of one. It recognizes human transcendence and the inevitable anomalies transcendence brings.

Anomalous monism: theological applications

Let us now appropriate some of the themes of anomalous monism and employ them analogically in theology and Christology. An immediate advantage of the theory when it becomes a theological analogy is that it allows for an appropriate confession of ignorance about the nature of mental and emotional states. It rarely happens that philosophical materialism provides Christian theology with a series of employable insights! Yet within the conceptual framework provided by science human agents are said to present themselves as anomalies, or, to use the more traditional term, mysteries. 'Mystery' here is given a quite precise signification. It is a term which must never be used as a veiled licence to say whatever one wants. The human agent, firmly fixed in a material universe, is the subject of psychological states which do not appear to fit into this same universe but are anomalies in respect to it. There is thus an unfathomability about the facts of human consciousness and a transcendence of the human agent over the cold application of causal laws. So the statement that persons are mysterious is a most unmysterious statement. On the human level, then, there are whole areas of our life which stubbornly refuse causal explanation, third-person observation and scientific objectification. A person's choices can transcend the most refined attempts to predict his or her behaviour. This is because persons are free.

Before we compare the mystery which is the active human agent with the mystery which is the Person of Christ, we might note that anomalous monism provides a fine model of transcendence for speaking of God and his providential activity towards the world. In the case of the divine agent, the anomaly model fruitfully suggests that God's activity in the world is unable to be adequately understood as that of an infinite external cause bringing about an internal finite effect or series of effects, because the action of God, like human actions, need not be detectable by an empirical causality. The unfathomability in the human case of the facts of consciousness and the impossibility of a purely physicalist account of intentionality provide us with a highly suitable analogue for the unfathomability of the mind and intentions of God. If human action cannot be satisfactorily explained by causal reasoning, we are already primed to expect no less difficulty in explaining the actions of God. Creation, providence, miracle and the completion of creation through Christ are all to be located in 'agency-talk' which will be expected to display the quality of mystery or anomaly to which we have grown accustomed in the human case. In the divine case the degree of transcendence will be greatly heightened, and our confidence in God's actions will not be undermined by our inability to grasp how his actions proceed. Belief in God's action through creation, providence and the like is what makes the universe ultimately meaningful for us, because (in Swinburne's semi-technical phrase) a 'personal explanation' will have been provided for it. [29]

None the less it is the analogy between the human person and the Person of Christ that chiefly concerns us. When the account provided by anomalous monism of a person's conscious states is compared with what Christians believe about the divine Person of Christ, the first striking feature of the comparison is that even on the human level there is a baffling mystery, coupled with an extreme immediacy about how both conscious states and their relation to physical states are understood. The anomaly model reminds us that there is much going on within finite being, especially at the human level, which transcends empirical discernment. The range of subjective experiences had by persons are importantly opaque to attempts to understand them by means of scientific, law-governed explanations. That is the meaning of 'anomalous'. Theologians often make pleas for cognitive humility when dealing with their peculiar subject-matter, but here is a case where cognitive humility is required long before the theologian comes on the scene. The presence of mystery at the everyday personal level helps us to adopt an appropriate attitude of cognitive humility towards the Person of Christ. Human beings are not generally disposed to tolerate ignorance, and ignorance of an area of life so immediate and basic to the experience of being a person is often dismissed as unthinkable instead of being frankly recognized and incorporated into a more tentative framework. When applied to the Person of Christ the theory also primes us to expect unfathomability, together with the breakdown of discourse involving causes, origins, hypotheses, and so on. In referring to the being of God in Christ as a mystery, the Church does not need to be oversensitive about its inability to provide a rational/causal type of account of the mysteries of the faith, such as, for example, how the eternal Son of God became incarnate in the womb of the *Theotocos*. The ontological unfathomability which is every human person, a mystery unresolved and undissolved by our familiarity with and immediacy to it, may provide an appropriate grounding for our understanding of the ontological unfathomability of the Person of Christ.

The analogy between the human person and the Person of Christ is being used here to indicate that the acute philosophical difficulties which attend the positing of a human subject, the person, have as their analogates the acute theological difficulties which attend the positing of a metaphysical subject, the divine Person of Christ. A merit of anomalous monism is its recognition of the difficulties. On the theological side there also stands a transcendental subject, this time the triune God who in one of his Persons has become fully revealed in, and completely a part of, the physical, historical world. The transcendence of this unique divine subject stands not only outside the grasp of science and philosophy but outside time and space altogether, while becoming incarnate in both. Faced with a problem of such magnitude, analogy is the best method available to human thought because illustration, not resolution, is all that can be attempted. But at least one can be clear about what one is attempting to illustrate. On the human level anomalous monism illustrates that when persons try to account for their freedom, for that which constitutes them as persons, they cannot 'deliver the goods', for science and philosophy (as Williams concedes) alike break down. In the circumstances, it is better to live without answers than to live with spurious ones.

How might anomalous monism provide some analogical insights into the issues of Christ's divine omnipotence and consciousness? Jesus is a divine agent, he is God incarnate, and we can carry over one of our conclusions from chapter 4, that between Jesus and God there is both 'identity of reference' and 'difference of meaning'.[30] The incarnate Christ remains 'truly God' while the meaning or manifestation of his Godhood during his incarnate life is allowed to differ from what it might be eternally in the Godhead. The analogy helps us to speculate, within an appropriate framework of reverent ignorance, that Jesus possessed, in comparison with us, enhanced powers or properties. It is appropriate to speak of at least the properties of enhanced freedom, power, knowledge and consciousness. We cannot know directly whether Jesus had an enhanced freedom, since we have no first-person perspective on his consciousness, but we do have a basic model which allows us to speculate that he might have had. The analogy illustrates that Jesus may have been genuinely 'anomalous' with respect to other (sinful) human beings, so that enhanced powers, where Scripture indicates he possessed them, are entirely justifiable. Since human agency is itself mysterious, and since Jesus is both human and divine, we may expect his powers of agency, i.e. his freedom, to exceed what, from a third-person perspective, we are able to predict, infer or calculate. His Person is a mystery, and while we might think that he mostly operated within our human limitations there is no requirement on us to think that he always did so.

Christians should not expect Jesus to have possessed arbitrary powers of agency such as are ascribed to him by the apocryphal gospels. But is it too much to expect that the One who was a unique divine/human subject, inscrutable to us, really did, for example, heal lepers, cure paralysis and restore a withered hand (Mark 1.40–3.6)? Must we simply accept, even in the special case of the incarnation, that only what is causally explicable is believable? We should not expect Jesus to have had a knowledge of the details of evolutionary theory or nuclear physics, but why should we not suppose that he had an enhanced knowledge of his Father, of his friends, of the people who came to hear him or to be healed or rebuked by him, together with their deepest needs and motives, and many other matters unknown to us? We do not know much about what Jesus knew and did not know, but we ought not to be surprised if the range or depth of his knowledge was enhanced in relation to ours. We do, however, know enough about human brains to speculate that whatever Jesus did know could be 'stored' in his brain, and not in a separate divine mind.

In a similar way, we may also speak of the enhanced consciousness of Jesus. I argued in the previous chapter that it is appropriate to speak of him, as part of our overall description, as a person with a human consciousness. He had a human will. Yet to say this is not to say enough about the mystery of his Person, for he was also God incarnate, and the will of God incarnate is divine. But being God incarnate amounts to doing the Father's will in just the way Jesus did it. At Gethsemane he surrendered his own will to that of the Father (Mark 14.36). The anomalous subject who is God the Son may as God have come to own human suffering and dereliction, and as a human person he may have come to know the full splendour of union with the Father. But obedience to God's will as a human person is of course not the same thing as possessing God's will because one already has a divine nature. In the latter case the question of obedience or disobedience could scarcely arise. I have already indicated in chapters 4 and 5 that the language of complementarity provides the best solution to the problem of two minds, two consciousnesses, and so on. The experience of being a person actually demands that complementary languages be spoken. In the case of the divine Person of Christ that demand is yet more insistent. But any suggestion of a double-consciousness in Christ, with its inevitable connotation of a split-personality, is best avoided.

Another advantage of anomalous monism as a theological model is that it provides a *via negativa* for Christology and it grounds it in our experience of being a reflective human agent. Whenever we seek to arrive at a settled account of the divine incarnate subject, the mystery of his incarnate being eludes us. The analogy illustrates that even in the human case the elusiveness of subjectivity forces our language about it to break down. Language is overwhelmed by the ontological depth of the human self. Christians who describe Jesus of Nazareth as God's ingenerate Son, the eternal God uniting the temporal world to himself by a gracious incarnate act, push the limits of language still further back. They too are confronted by an ontological depth which their most inspired thoughts can penetrate only partly. The analogy provides a further opportunity for emphasizing the unity of the human person as a single subject of physical and psychological states which are different states while remaining rooted in the anomaly which is the human agent. The value of the analogy for Christology is that it helps us to anchor a great mystery in a lesser mystery, yet one which is also intimately known to us.

The limits of analogy

What is the most obvious disanalogy here? The basic series of analogies in this book from chapter 3 onwards starts with the unity *within* the human person. The christological problem (as I have presented it) is, on the other hand, about the unity of God (the Son) *with* a human person which is already a unity of body and mind, or physical and psychological states, etc. In classical christological terms, the Word was united not merely with flesh but with complete manhood.[31] So on one side of the analogy there is an internal unity, that of the human person; on the other side there is an external unity of God, between the divine Person of the Son and the human person of Jesus. On the human side a person is a single complex unity of body and mind; on the divine side there is a unity of God with what has already been defined as a unity of body and mind. The 'supervenience' (as we might term it) of the divine Person upon the human person constitutes a new and divine unity of different parts and may even be thought to disrupt the unity which operates on the purely human level.

It is important to say what the basic analogy between the individual person and the Person of the divine Son can and cannot do. The analogy makes no attempt to establish that the divine Person of Christ became incarnate at all. The analogy *does* however attempt to show that, if God graciously chose to become incarnate in Jesus of Nazareth, then we are able to understand that he has done so. This is what the Christian faith encourages us to think, and one important aid to our understanding is the knowledge we have of the mysterious unities we ourselves are simply by being human persons. The analogy is limited to suggesting that the holy mystery which is the incarnation of God in Christ is partially illuminated by the mystery which is every developed human being.

The believing human mind, then, has a genuine knowledge of the mystery of Christ. And inasmuch as this knowledge is human and partial, it is transcended by the mystery it comprehends, and the human mind thus knows itself to be in the presence of transcending mystery. Part of the human knowledge of God in Christ is a realization that once we try to probe it descriptions, causes, even reasons, finally give out. The mind is then left, we might say, to adore the holy and let itself be shaped by it, and this is what happens in Christian worship. We have identified the point at which the analogy between the human person and the divine person breaks down, but this is hardly an objection to the analogical method which has been adopted, for all analogies eventually break down. We may speculate that the human consciousness of Jesus, being unseparated from God by sin, was unique in its direct acquired knowledge of the Father. We may also speculate that the incarnate Christ continued in the mutual interrelation of love between the divine Persons which existed from eternity. And we may speculate that the Godhead was conscious of being incarnate in the Person of the Son. Anomalous monism cannot help us confirm these speculations, but it can coax us into a confident and helpful agnosticism in the face of arguments about the precise constitution of the incarnate Christ, for we are now aware of the acute philosophical difficulties involved in adopting a third-person perspective on the contents of anyone's consciousness at all. In short, there is another kind of unity with which human beings are intimately acquainted, which is itself a mystery transcending attempts to comprehend it. It is the unity of mind and body in the human person which gives us a model for understanding the divine mystery of the Word made man. So we do possess, as the early fathers recognized, some means of imagining what it might be like for there to be a unity between God and Jesus which is importantly similar to the unity which we experience as persons. And that unity is redescribed in the next chapter, where the 'whole person' is compared with the Person of God the Son.

NOTES

1 Thomas V. Morris, *The Logic of God Incarnate* (Ithaca and London: Cornell University Press, 1986), p. 89; see also pp. 88–107.
2 ibid., pp. 102–7; see also above, p. 47.
3 ibid., p. 104.
4 ibid., pp. 142, 144.
5 ibid., p. 150.
6 Above, pp. 47–8.
7 Morris, *The Logic of God Incarnate*, pp. 161–2.
8 Dietrich Bonhoeffer, *Christology* (London: Collins, 1966, pp. 108–9.
9 Peter Geach elicited some robust responses when he claimed that 'no graspable sense has ever been given' to the sentence 'God can do everything' which 'did not lead to self-contradiction or at least to conclusions manifestly untenable from the Christian point of view'. See Peter Geach, *Providence and Evil* (Cambridge: Cambridge University Press, 1977), p. 4.
10 See Thomas P. Flint and Alfred J. Freddoso, 'Maximal Power' in Thomas V. Morris (ed.), *The Concept of God* (Oxford: Oxford University Press, 1987). The authors defend their definition (p. 156) against several others, including Geach, Swinburne and Plantinga.
11 J. L. Mackie, 'Evil and Omnipotence' in Basil Mitchell (ed.), *The Philosophy of Religion* (Oxford: Oxford University Press, 1971). (Mackie revises the argument in his *The Miracle of Theism* (Oxford: Clarendon Press, 1982), p. 160.)
12 e.g. Emil Brunner, *The Christian Doctrine of God*. tr. O. Wyon (London: Lutterworth, 5th imp., 1962), pp. 248–55. Process theologians unanimously reject omnipotence as an attribute of God, qualifying God's power as the power of Love.
13 Stephen T. Davis elaborates this contrast in his *Logic and the Nature of God* (London and Basingstoke: Macmillan, 1983), pp. 122–31.
14 Morris, *The Logic of God Incarnate*, pp. 99–101.
15 Brunner, *The Christian Doctrine of God*, p. 248, 250.

16 ibid., p. 254.
17 Above p. 55.
18 e.g. Norman Pittenger, *Christology Reconsidered* (London: S C M Press, 1970), ch. 7.
19 Above, pp. 85–6.
20 Brian Hebblethwaite, *The Incarnation* (Cambridge: Cambridge University Press, 1987), p. 31.
21 ibid., p. 164.
22 I am grateful to John Macquarrie for this point.
23 Donald Davidson, 'Psychology as Philosophy' in Jonathan Glover (ed.), *The Philosophy of Mind* (Oxford: Oxford University Press, 1976), p. 103.
24 Donald Davidson, 'Mental Events' in L. Foster and J. W. Swanson (eds), *Experience and Theory* (Cambridge, Mass.: University of Massachusetts Press, 1970), pp. 87, 101.
25 Davidson, 'Psychology as Philosophy', p. 102.
26 Alasdair MacIntyre, *After Virtue* (London: Duckworth, 1981), ch. 8.
27 Bernard Williams, *Descartes: The Project of Human Enquiry* (Harmondsworth: Pelican Books, 1978), ch. 10, 'Mind and its Place in Nature', p. 295, author's emphasis. See also pp. 295–7.
28 Above, pp. 71–2.
29 Richard Swinburne, *The Existence of God* (Oxford: Clarendon Press, 1979), ch. 2.
30 Above, pp. 49–50.
31 Above, p. 26.

CHAPTER 9

Whole Persons

In the previous chapter the analogy between the human person and the divine Person was supplemented by the theory of anomalous monism and important insights were added to our analogical approach to the Person of Christ. In this chapter the material for the analogical approach to the Person of Christ is provided by those accounts of persons which emphasize their wholeness. The material will be called the 'organic model'. To speak of something as organic is to suggest that it is living and so capable of growth, and that it is a whole or unity which imposes form on its parts. An organic model of persons locates them in their evolutionary history. But we should also recall the warning of John Macmurray that 'an organic conception of the personal is inadequate to the facts', because the form of the truly personal is found 'only through the mutuality of personal relationship'.[1] The social concept of the person will be brought into our series of analogies in chapter 10. Despite its limitations, the organic model, together with its biological basis, will extend and conclude our series of analogies based on the individual person. It will enable some remarks to be made about the origins of Jesus, his eternal generation and virginal birth. And it will be used to make important suggestions about the uniqueness and sinlessness of Jesus.

The organic model

The contrast between a whole and its parts is ancient, and is reminiscent of the contrast between the one and the many in Plato's *Parmenides*. The category mistake which Ryle's illustration of the foreigner visiting Oxford or Cambridge exposed[2] was a confusion between a whole and its parts. 'University' and 'colleges' are related to each other as a whole is related to parts, despite their deceptive grammatical appearance as belonging to the same *genus*. The illustration is also a reminder that the real cannot be reduced to the merely observable. The foreigner was correct in expecting to find a university and incorrect only in the expectation of what a university was. Once he had realized the University was a whole made up of different parts he would not be expected to speak of it as if only the parts were 'really there'. Other illustrations of wholes transcending parts are commonplace. Buildings, industrial machines, musical compositions and even fish fingers all impose unities on the parts of which they consist and cannot be reduced to a random arrangement of them. But the most striking example of a whole transcending its parts is the living human organism. The human mind, according to the organic view of persons is certainly not a substance apart from matter, but, again, it is not nothing either. It is possible to say that the human organism just is a conscious unity, and that there is no need to introduce the term 'mind' in order to refer to that feature of its life. I have retained it because it is a convenient way of drawing attention to the self-consciousness of the human organism as a whole and because the authors on whom I am about to draw have retained it too. It does not require a Cartesian framework in order to have a use. Rather its relation to body (if we may still speak of relation) *is* the relation between a whole and its parts. The emphasis on wholeness is of course an emphasis on the integration of all the components of the human organism into a living unity, so the example of a living unity which each of us is in being a person is our starting-point for thinking about the unity of the Person of Christ.

Our first example of holism is taken from one of the greatest biologists of the century, Theodosius Dobzhansky. Like all present-day biologists he has no use for any doctrine of vitalism, which posits a vital force external to living things, nor for an entelechy, which was once thought somehow to direct their development. Theologians are also warned by Dobzhansky against panpsychism, the view that 'all matter has in it some rudiments of life, feeling, and volition'.[3] It is true that 'the potentiality of mind must have been present in the protoplasm'[4] but it does not follow from this, he says, that mind or any factor remotely analogous to mind was present there. Biologists can make no sense of supernatural agency, and it is 'most certainly difficult, perhaps quite impossible', to reconstruct how humankind came to acquire its distinctive physiological and anatomical features.[5] There is no unbridgeable gap between the *humanum* and the prehuman state'; rather the distinctiveness of the *humanum* is the product of a rearrangement, of a new unity, of prehuman life. 'Now', he continues,

> the point which the believers in unbridgeable gaps miss is that the qualitative novelty of the human estate is the novelty of a pattern, not of its components. The transcendence does not mean that a new force or energy has arrived from nowhere; it does mean that *a new form of unity* has come into existence. At all events, no component of the *humanum* can any longer be denied to animals, although the human constellation of these components certainly can.[6]

Once we recall that the Chalcedonian fathers were concerned with not merely the two natures of Christ but their unity,[7] references to 'a new form of unity' in the human case may offer at last a hint of a possible analogy between the organic model of a person and Christ's Person.

We are now in a better position to develop what is meant by advocating that a person be understood as a whole transcending the sum of its parts. All compound substances are wholes consisting of parts, so thus far nothing distinctive has been said. However, against the background of its evolutionary past, the unity of the person stands out as a 'qualitative novelty' which accords well with what has been claimed for the concept 'person' already. Dualism is not required to explain the distinctiveness of persons (no 'new force or energy has arrived from nowhere'). Reductionism is also avoided. 'Quite literally', observes Dobzhansky, 'man is a conglomeration of transformed groceries.' A bolder materialist statement would be hard to find, yet it is soon qualified, and its purpose is shown to be not to devalue humankind in a hierarchy of beings but to revalue the material world from which humankind comes and to which it belongs. 'This conglomeration is, however, alive, feels joy and suffering, possesses consciousness and self-awareness, and is capable of deeds ranging from kindness to knavery and from heroism to egoism.'[8] P-predicates, we might say, are still capable of ascription to the human physical organism, whose transcendence is unthreatened by being treated as a higher unity or 'constellation of components'.

The *humanum*, then, is a unique whole of parts within the organic world. The traditional name for this type of view is holism. It is well known that the parts or organs of a living whole are divisible into smaller sub-parts or sub-systems; for example, a human body has many organs, and each of them is further subdivisible into tissues, which are then further subdivisible into cells, then into chromosomes, genes and molecules. And the new particle physics now enables us to go far beyond the molecular level to the sub-atomic level where physical reality further subdivides into nuclei and electrons, nucleons, quarks, and the like. The holistic approach to persons invites application not merely downwards towards the sub-systems of the human body but outwards towards groups of people, existing socially and bound together by common interests, loyalties, aims and the like. The social application of the organic model doubtless owes something to metaphor, but may be validly made, as for example when the Christian Church is called 'the body of Christ'. The term 'organization' picks up the social application, like the term 'system', for when it is used metaphorically of commercial businesses (*organizations*) or the formal ordering or arranging of social or political activities (becoming 'organ-ized') the root biological origin of the term is carried over. In the biological 'home territory' of the concept, discrete entities combine together to produce organized wholes which in turn give them form, as a football team may be said by analogy to be an organization or system of individual players, a machine an organized system of parts and the solar system an organization of planets.

Organicism, then, is non-dualist and non-reductionist while at the same time emphasizing the unity of the physical organism. A second and final example of an organic view of persons is taken from that distinguished book *Creation and the World of Science* by the biochemist and theologian Arthur Peacocke. He holds that 'the language describing mental events is not reducible to that of cerebral physico-chemical events'. Rather

> mental activity and functions, 'consciousness', may be regarded as a genuinely emergent feature at that level in the hierarchy of complexity which is the human brain in the human body . . . The newness of the activity and function are real enough, but these are not an activity and function of some new thing or entity, the 'mind', but are a new activity and function of the all-pervasive physico-chemical units that emerges when these units have evolved a particular kind of organized complexity . . . Mental activity does not necessarily have to be predicated of some new entity, the 'mind', which is, as it were, added as a new kind of order of being to the neurological network of physico-chemical structures and processes which constitute the brain . . . One can be anti-reductionist about mental processes and events and 'anti-mentalist', in the sense of not postulating an entity called the 'mind'.[9]

Organic or 'organicist' accounts of the person are biologically based, yet they blend convincingly with the conclusions of the conceptual work done by Strawson and Davidson. Let us now see what insights may be gained by comparing the organic model of a person with Christian teaching about the Person of Christ. The accounts show that, in the human case, both dualism and vitalism are simply unnecessary in accounting for the place of human consciousness in the world. Ryle's illustration depicted the confusion that can arise when a whole is mistakenly understood as one more part. But the accounts of persons described in this chapter do not allow any reductive slide either, for the evolutionary novelty of the human species is defined by means of a higher unification and organization of living, emergent matter. We do not weaken Christian belief in the deity of Christ if deity is predicated of Christ as a whole; indeed by doing so a central theme of Christology is recovered, viz. the unity of Christ's Person, whose divine and human natures are 'without separation'.

The biological grounding of the whole and parts analogy gives form to an approach to the Person of Christ which also relates divinity to humanity as a whole to parts. But the whole on the human side of the analogy is the conscious living organism; on the

Godward side of the analogy stands the divine Person. How is the wholeness of this Person to be depicted, and of what parts may we say the wholeness consists? The analogy looks to be inappropriate, even inapplicable, given the vast differences between the eternal Son and the frail human organism. However, even here there are elements of the organic account which help us to grasp something of the being of God-in-person, and to make sense of the different traditions regarding our Lord's human origins.

The organic model and the whole Christ

The organic model of the person lets us understand the human mind or consciousness as a unification or integration of many parts. The mind is not nothing, but it is not a 'pure subject' (Strawson's phrase) either. Let us now say the mind *is* the total integration of the 'parts' of the body, or, better, of the parts of the person itself. 'Parts' here includes not merely the many organs, systems and sub-systems of the body, the continuous sensory stimulation the body receives and the responses to them, but the integration of past and future through memory and rational action, and the integration of reason and feeling, of duty and desire, of responsibility and freedom. The analogy is still not wide enough, for personal being is unsustainable without relationships with others, and these too can be characterized by degrees of integration and disintegration. The whole is the living person in all its parts, which at the same time transcends them. The analogy with the Person of Christ suggests that the divine *hypostasis*, God the Son, and the human person, Jesus of Nazareth, are perfectly one, as a whole and its parts are potentially one in the organic model. Paul Tillich has used the metaphor of 'centredness' to illustrate the effect of the person's integrating of the totality of his or her experiences. 'The personal centre', he observes, 'is not identical with any one of the psychological contents, but neither is it another element added to them.'[10] In the case of Jesus, God is the whole or centre. The Father does not replace the personal centre of Jesus; rather the integration of Jesus with himself (i.e. all the elements of his person) and his integration with other persons (i.e. in relationships, some of them conflictual) presents a whole or unity which is also a unity between God himself and an open, perfect, human life.

If the organic model prompts a suggestion about the being of Jesus, what might it suggest about his origins? Chalcedon confesses the divine Son 'begotten of the Father before the ages as touching the Godhead, the same in the last days, for us and for our salvation, born from the Virgin Mary, the *Theotocos*, as touching the manhood'. The statement is an excellent example of the use of double languages referring to the one subject, one language primarily theological in purpose, the other primarily historical, yet each incomplete and misleading without qualification by the other. When an organic understanding of the person is brought to the person Jesus of Nazareth, his complete solidarity with all living beings is clearly emphasized. Jesus, as St Luke records (with some other rival view in mind?), was 'the son, as people thought, of Joseph' (Luke 3.23). Jesus, we may safely say, had a human birth! Only so can we agree that he was 'truly man' or 'completely human'. But recent advances in biology give a startling new emphasis to the real physicality of Jesus. Jesus, it has been ably said, had 'all the pre-history of man in his genes', for 'to be a member of the species *homo sapiens* includes genes and chromosomes shaped and trans-mitted by millions of years of evolution'.[11] The recent discovery of DNA and RNA, and the attendant microscopic level of life, helps us to understand at a level inconceivable to the Chalcedonian fathers what it might be like for Jesus to be 'one in being with us as touching the manhood'. The One who is confessed as the complete embodiment of the fullness of Godhead is one and the same as the historical person who stands in complete solidarity with all living creatures, and is made up of precisely the same 'building blocks of life' as we are. The biological solidarity of Jesus with the human species, and through the human species to the older pre-human antecedents, emphasizes the fitness of the organic world which is created by God to be also the bearer of his very being.

When interpreting the virginal birth of Jesus two extremes are to be avoided. One gives the same status to the doctrine of the virgin birth as it gives to the other legends of which the birth narratives of Matthew and Luke are full. On this view the doctrine is little more than a fable, void of real content, yet a picturesque way of making a theological point about God's initiatory action in 'sending' Jesus. The other extreme regards the birth narratives as containing literal descriptions of the miraculous origin of Jesus (Matthew 1.20; Luke 1.35). If parthenogenesis were possible, so the argument runs, the offspring conceived apart from any male sharing in the conception would be female because she would lack a Y chromosome. This lack, however, far from being an argument against partheno-genesis, becomes instead evidence for supernatural intervention in the birth of Jesus, for the conception of Jesus was non-natural, and the Y chromosome which gives Jesus his maleness is provided by supernatural intervention.[12] It is hard to say which is the worse alternative, for both approaches begin with the questionable premise of the literalness of the birth narratives; one then goes on to argue that the literalness is mistaken, and that like the massacre of innocent children at Bethlehem (Matthew 2.16–18) or the sing-ing of the heavenly choir (Luke 2.13) it owes more to imagination than fact; the other makes the literalness of the accounts an essen-tial safeguard of Jesus' divinity. The first alternative robs the doctrine of its theological significance; the second makes the theo-logical significance dependent on an empirical hypothesis (about a delicate and private matter – the conception of a child). The mid-dle ground to be preferred is again a moderate realism, and the whole and parts analogy developed in this chapter provides clues in suggesting how this middle position might be developed.

The organic accounts of a person just discussed all assume that persons are novel unities of organic material which surpass in ability and complexity pre-human species. The origin of the human species, then, lies in unbroken continuity with earlier pre-human species. This is of course an assumption, for the record is fragmen-tary, but it is a thoroughly plausible one.[13] Evolution has produced genuinely novel devleopments which could not have been predict-ed in advance, but which retrospectively make sense as novel de-velopments from more primitive beings. Thus we arrive at the commonplace position that the world which evolutionary theory attempts to explain is one where there are already many inexplica-ble jumps, false starts and breath-taking advances. In affirming, as they must, the non-natural origin of the human Jesus, Christians assert that the totality which Jesus was cannot be finally described in natural or causal ways. With regard to human biological origins, evolutionary theory invites, even compels, us to assume unpredict-able organic advances which cannot yet be satisfactorily explained. The doctrine of our Lord's birth from a virgin mother safeguards his uniqueness, not because it gives God the Holy Spirit the super-natural task of providing the missing Y chromosome, but because it expresses the growing conviction of the early Church that no human person is in principle capable of attaining that manifesta-tion of God-ness which it perceives to have occurred in Jesus.

The qualitative gap between Jesus and ourselves need not there-fore be threatened by applying an organic analogy to him, for the very gaps we have noted in the evolutionary story give the analogi-cal prompting we might need to prepare ourselves for that un-bridgeable gap between God the Son and ourselves, between him who is without sin and the rest of us. Christians are, and are not, 'believers in unbridgeable gaps' (Dobzhansky's phrase). There is no organic discontinuity between Jesus and ourselves; rather the gap is to be discerned at the point of comparison between the total pattern of his life, where God is at the centre and is the unifying whole, and the total pattern of ours, where the centre is distorted by sin and partiality. Jesus cannot be interpreted simply and solely as a 'natural' or 'historical' phenomenon, even though he certainly occurs in nature and history. Neither are a few more million years of human evolution likely to throw up an individual who approxi-mates to the goodness and perfection of God's eternal Son.

Jesus Christ is not merely born of a virgin, but is also eternally begotten of the Father. Here we may need to be reminded that in our everyday experience of other persons we do not have access to their minds and intentions, only to their bodily performances. By the same token, we cannot hope to have access to the mind and intentions of God; what we do have, however, is Jesus Christ and the fullness of God through him. Wittgenstein's warning against adopting the picture theory of language is especially apt in the case of both the miraculous birth and the divine generation. In one case the mistaken picture conjures up an absent human father, an incomprehensible event (miraculous parthenogenesis) and a mistaken description which is more clinical than theological in character. In the other, the mistaken picture is that of a pre-temporal beginning to the eternal Son. Once we heed Wittgenstein's warning that descriptions 'are instruments for particular uses',[14] then 'begotten of the Father' and 'born from the Virgin Mary' can be reinstated as truth-conveying descriptions which jointly express and protect the divinity and humanity of the one Jesus Christ and take the causal questions implied in both to their limits.

A new pattern of personalness

The organic model is applicable also to Christian claims about the uniqueness and sinlessness of Christ. It suggests that our knowledge of the divine Person be understood as the revelation of a new pattern of personalness, an interpretation fully consistent with the gospel record. The uniqueness of the human species *vis-à-vis* other species lies in a new configuration of the biological material, not in the emergence of a species which produced a non-biological counterpart in addition to its biological inheritance. In like manner Christian theology can claim that what makes the Christ unique among humankind is also (borrowing Dobzhansky's words) 'the novelty of a pattern', a pattern or whole which while fully, biologically human manifests itself personally and socially. The uniqueness of the human species comes about by an evolutionary jump or series of jumps; the uniqueness of the Person of Christ comes about by the intervention and self-giving of God.

Jesus was confessed as the Christ by the early Church because of, *inter alia*, the new pattern of human life which emerged historically through him. If his historical life, and not merely his organic being, is regarded as the 'whole', then the 'parts' of this whole include his intentions and actions, viz. his teachings, his thoughts and feelings, his sublime love of God and humankind, his passionate concern for justice, his deep openness to others, his sufferings, death and resurrection. Most of his actions are unknown to us; some of his thoughts and feelings would have remained unknown even to his closest disciples. But, taken together, the known and the unknown were believed to comprise a totality which, when apprehended for what it is, compelled the ascription of Godhood to him, in faith and absolute commitment.

The unique ontological reality of the Christ is upheld and confessed by what were called D-predicates,[15] but why are these predicates ascribed by Christians exclusively to Jesus and no other person? The Godhood of Jesus is not merely a property of his humanhood. But the unity of his Godhood and his humanhood in his one historical life enabled his Godhood to be recognized through his humanhood. According to the Chalcedonian definition Jesus is 'perfect in manhood' (*teleion . . . en anthropoteti*), and 'of one substance with us as touching the manhood'. Jesus had long been regarded as 'truly man', and one reason for stating this rather obvious truism was to rule out an early heresy, docetism, which denied the real humanity of Jesus. In an anti-docetic context the force of the affirmation that Jesus is 'truly a human being' lies in the denial that Jesus only *appeared* to be a human being. But another reason for saying that Jesus was truly a human being was to affirm that Jesus was more truly human than anyone else. And now something more than full membership of the human species is being asserted. What is now meant is that in Jesus Christ Christians claim to see what true humanness is, what true personhood means.

'Perfect in manhood' may be fairly translated 'completely a person' or 'complete in regard to his humanity'. We have already noted how, for Morris, the full humanity of Jesus may amount to no more than his having one or two human properties, like having a human body and a human consciousness.[16] Of course (following Morris) the phrase 'perfectly man' or 'perfect in manhood' can be misleadingly construed to suggest that Jesus was scarcely a man at all, but a God-Man with little or no connecting links with the rest of us. But what the phrase conveys instead is that Jesus was completely a human being and that as a human being he was more completely or fully a human being than anyone else. And that is what is meant by a 'new pattern of personalness' or 'new form of unity'. In this sense Jesus is the revelation of personhood. He is 'the norm of what a truly human existence should be'.[17] The speculative question, what it might be like to be completely a person, has as its non-speculative answer: Jesus Christ. Jesus Christ is the definitive pattern of personalness for Christians. They believe that 'God in and through Jesus has afforded us a new interpretation of personalness, a new definition . . . of what it is, or rather might be, to be human'.[18] If a human being is to become 'completely a person', salvation and much sanctification is needed. Jesus in his historical life exemplifed what being completely a person means. Thus the teaching of Jesus about the need for unconditional love of one's neighbour, say, or his forgiveness of his executioners, his

intolerance of hypocrisy and cant, his remarkable understanding
and acceptance of other people (Zacchaeus, the woman at the well,
the woman caught in adultery), even his death as a self-enacted
parable of vulnerability and openness; these are some of the brush
strokes which paint the picture of Jesus as the revelation of true
personalness.[19]

The wholeness and sinlessness of Chirst

The organic model of a person, with its stress on unity and wholeness, can clarify and develop the fundamental doctrine of human
sinfulness and the Chalcedonian statement that the Christ is 'like
us in all things apart from sin'. One way among others of recover-
ing the meaning of the doctrine of sin, and Christ's claimed exemp-
tion from it, is to emphasize the condition of salvation as 'wholeness' or 'being made whole'. Salvation is then the integration of the
different elements of the person in fullness of life; sin the disruption
of these elements leading to disintegration and even destruction.
The Greek verb *sozein*, 'to heal' or 'to save', is connected with *sos*
(saos), 'whole' or 'sound', and so has an original meaning 'to render whole, sound'. The Authorized Version of the Bible often ren-
ders *sozein* as 'to make whole', as for example, when Jesus says to
the woman with the haemorrhage, 'Daughter, thy faith hath made
thee whole; go in peace, and be whole of thy plague' (Mark 5.34).
Sozein in the New Testament emphasizes the centrality of organic
wholeness for understanding the work of Christ, for its primary
biblical use is in the context of physical illness and the restoration
to health. Only then is physical salvation made the occasion for
linking wholeness more widely with the general human condition.

Some of the concepts discussed in chapter 1 also have a contribution to make to the commendation of Jesus as the bringer of a
new pattern of personalness. The psychological concept of a person picked out the process of unfolding, which reveals itself in the
acquisition of character. The Gospels enable us to point to events
in our Lord's life (e.g. his temptations, his decision to go to
Jerusalem) where his resoluteness indicates his unwillingness to be
deflected from his messianic mission, and where the strength of
character which he acquires through soul-searching and struggle
enables him to accept his arrest and death as submission to his
Father's will. Jesus, as a cursory look at the Gospels shows, clearly
regarded other people as 'ends in themselves' (in accordance with
the moral concept of a person). Equally the possibility of understanding his life as a 'project' which he actualizes in freedom and
for which he takes complete responsibility (the existential concept
of a person), is striking. Sartre's lonely individual who is condemned to be free and cannot not be responsible for every act he or
she engages in does not look a promising model for understanding

Jesus. None the less Christians may observe that only the person who was also God the Son could carry the burden of freedom that Sartre puts upon us, and that this person did actually shoulder it in God's name and for God's sake. For Sartre, as for Kant, mere obedience to an external authority requires neither freedom nor responsibility. It is just heteronomy. But the project which was the completed life of Jesus is invulnerable to this criticism. For Jesus first takes responsibility for choosing what is the will of God for his life before he carries it out. He has a new understanding of what obedience to the will of God amounts to.

Sin, then, can be characterized as the condition that inhibits wholeness, which works instead towards the disruption of the individual and his or her essential unity. It may be possible to widen 'disruption' to include the disruption of purpose, where 'weakness of will' has an acquired effect on the development of character; the disruption of relationships, where, for selfish advantage, other people are used for one's own ends; and the disruption of resolve, where the person is overcome by, for example, a lack of meaning to his or her life. The biological basis for talk about wholeness and disruption (and eventual disintegration) is instructive, for the effects of sin on individuals and social groups are comparable to the effects of the intrusion of a virus or a disease into a living organism, disrupting and affecting the whole in a negative and potentially disintegrative way. An individual human body is itself a 'society' of limbs and organs, and the interdependence of each upon the other is well known, so if a single limb or organ malfunctions the organism as a whole is affected, and its performance as a whole is likely to be impaired. The organic model can be naturally extended to include even the human race itself, for there too humankind can be seen collectively as a single global society of nations and cultures which, instead of enriching and supporting each other as co-partners in the universal Kingdom of God, are largely turned against each other in disintegrative activity.

A similar charge of disintegration may be laid against the relationship between human beings and all other beings ('man' and 'nature'). The metaphor 'sin', then, powerfully draws attention to the actual human condition, both individually and socially. The individual may find the impulses of, for example, possessiveness, competitiveness, uncaringness and selfishness too strong, and they may threaten to distort his or her fragile unity by 'pulling him in all directions at once'. Socially, the wider human society is threatened with 'dis-integration' and is divided against itself in several ways which are open to empirical study. Individually and socially, salvation is the experience of integration and wholeness; sin the tendency towards disintegration and division.

When the Christ is confessed as the One who was 'one in being with us as touching the manhood, like us in all things apart from sin', one may be confident that Jesus was seen from the earliest times as manifesting in his human life the singular absence of those tendencies which disrupt and pervert human existence in its essential unity. In the historical life of Jesus of Nazareth one may expect to find an absence of self-interest, acquisitiveness, greed, envy, exploitation, hypocrisy, and the like, which marks him out as a person sufficiently troublesome and unusual for the authorities to have wanted to silence him; and as a person who, perhaps by his immense and unfailing love for people, his understanding of their weaknesses, his defence of their rights, or his exposure of their oppressors, invited the response from the first believers that here was no ordinary man but one who came from God and was God. The historical totality of Christ's life was seen as revealing the one true God in the new unity which all its different parts created, a unity which flourished because those very features of humanness which would distort it were overcome in this one perfectly human life.

The organic model of persons has prompted suggestions about the being of God in Christ, its origins, uniqueness and perfection. In the next chapter the long-overdue examination of the *social* model of the person will be taken up.

NOTES

1   John Macmurray, *The Self as Agent* (London: Faber & Faber, 1957), pp. 37–8.
2   Above, p. 53.
3   Theodosius Dobzhansky, *The Biology of Ultimate Concern* (London and Glasgow: Collins, 1971), p. 27.
4   ibid., p. 29.
5   ibid., p. 54.
6   ibid., p. 58, emphasis added.
7   Above p. 27.
8   Dobzhansky, *The Biology of Ultimate Concern*, p. 25.
9   A. R. Peacocke, *Creation and the World of Science* (Oxford: Oxford University Press, 1979), pp. 120–1.
10   Paul Tillich, *Systematic Theology, Volume 3* (Digswell Place: Nisbet, 1964), p. 28.
11   John A. T. Robinson, *The Human Face of God* (London: S C M Press, 1973), pp. 42–3.
12   See E. L. Mascall, *Theology and the Gospel of Christ* (London: S P C K, 1977), pp. 131–3.
13   The story of evolution has been brought up to date and made entertainingly accessible by Richard Dawkins in his *The Blind Watchmaker* (London and Harmondsworth: Penguin Books, 1988), But Dawkins is understandably touchy about the way some theologians interpret evolution (see, e.g. pp. 37–41). I hope I am doing nothing remiss here. The possiblity of supernatural intervention is of little interest to biologists.
14   Above, p. 63.
15   Above, p. 35, *et passim*.

16 Above, pp. 47–8.
17 Robinson, *The Human Face of God*, p. 67.
18 Peacocke, *Creation and The World of Science*, p. 245.
19 Part of this paragraph can be found in my 'Learning to Become Persons – A Theological Approach to Educational Aims', *Scottish Journal of Theology*, xxxvi (1983), pp. 522–7.

CHAPTER 10

Human Communities and Divine Persons

The argument developed thus far in this book has been based on a series of analogies from the human person to the divine Person of Christ. As our theme has been the single divine Person of Christ it has been appropriate to consider approaches to the human person which emphasize, or begin with, human individuality. But persons are not simply individuals, they are also and fundamentally social beings. And the Person of Christ, according to Christians, is but one Person in a divine Trinity of Persons. Can the social or relational reality of human persons convey any analogical hints about the triune nature of God? Conversely, does the assertion of a Trinity of Persons in God reveal anything about the character of human persons as beings in relationship? In this chapter I shall work towards the cautious answer 'yes' to both questions. To begin with, what is meant by the *social* concept of a person must be described. Alternative models of the Trinity must then be noted before both sides of the analogy can be brought together.

Human persons-in-relation

First, I am making a charge which it would take another book to substantiate, viz. that the tradition of British empiricist philosophy has concentrated excessively upon the individual as an autonomous, independent, rational agent, while failing to appreciate that the individual is also largely constituted by others and cannot escape interaction with them. Only a tradition which wrenches the individual person from others could ever have invented the insoluble problem of the existence of other minds than one's own. Second, we have already noted in chapter 2 how Cartesian dualism, like its empiricist counterpart, so isolates the human person as a 'thinking thing' that even the body of the thinker can be doubted away along with the rest of the uncertain external world. With Descartes the foundations of 'that newly invented social institution, the individual'[1] are laid. Third, we may observe that once the starting-point for the exploration of the person is individuality separated from others, it becomes difficult if not impossible ever to arrive at a satisfactory understanding of community. For Jeremy Bentham 'the community is a fictitious *body*, composed of the individual persons who are considered as constituting as it were its *members*'.[2] Finally, we may note the social consequences of the undue weight given to individuality at the expense of community. Alasdair MacIntyre's magisterial work *After Virtue* charts the breakdown of the sense of a moral community where once the practice of virtue was possible. The hiatus produced by the loss of the communal sense produces a climate of selfishness and competition, often aggressive, which is allowed to dominate all forms of social, moral, legal, political and economic life.[3]

The concept of a person-in-relation offers a different starting-point,[4] and in chapter 1 it was designated the social or communitarian concept of the person. The social concept of the person need not conflict with the individual concepts of the person which have already been discussed; indeed, it is important to recognize that both individuality and sociality equally contribute, as a polarity, to human personhood, as I shall shortly show. The concepts stressing human individuality have been emphasized in this book only because its theme has been the single Person of Christ. The biblical basis for the social concept of the person may be found in the teaching of Jesus about the vine and the branches (John 15.5) or in St Paul's use of the metaphor of the human body and its members (1 Corinthians 12.12–27; Romans 12.4–6). There are plenty of alternatives to the dogmatic individualism which still dominates popular secular and religious thought, though none of them has been very successful in displacing it. Let us merely list a few of them in order to indicate the range (to say nothing of the richness) of what is available.

G.W.F. Hegel's idealism provides one such alternative. His concept of Mind or *Geist* embraces all particular minds which are but different manifestations of the one cosmic, universal Mind.[5] The idealist philosopher F. H. Bradley spoke of the growing child as 'penetrated, infected, characterized by the existence of others. Its content implies in every fibre relations of community.'[6] A. N. Whitehead's philosophy of organism or process regards the individual human being as a 'society', not simply of limbs and organs, but of 'a serial succession of occasions of experience', with the result that, for Whitehead 'The Universe achieves its values by reason of its co-ordination into societies of societies, and into societies of societies of societies.'[7] The Marxist reaction to Hegel none the less retains an emphatic understanding of the human being as a *species being*.[8] In a different vein Martin Heidegger has attempted 'to *destroy* the history of ontology', excising on the way 'the *ego cogito* of Descartes, the subject, the "I", reason, spirit, person'.[9] While Heidegger cannot be straightforwardly enlisted in the 'communitarian camp', both his attack on the ossified ontology of the self and his attempt to shape a new vocabulary which articulates the basic state of human being or *Dasein* as 'being-in-the-world'[10] enable him to be identified as a fellow-traveller in the conquest of individualism.

Wittgenstein has done more than perhaps anyone to subvert the Cartesian notion of the mental ego with its autonomy and its privileged access to private inner states. Descartes' model of the self is a dangerously misleading one, which theologians are only just beginning to learn to resist.[11] We have seen in chapter 5 how what was called 'person language' is misused if it is understood to be straightforwardly describing inner states, and Fergus Kerr, who strongly endorses Wittgenstein's dissolution of the Cartesian 'I', comments, 'The point of exploring the private language fantasy is, then, to retrieve the natural expressiveness of the human body, *and to reaffirm the indispensability of belonging to a community*: two obvious facts that the metaphysically dictated conception of the self trivializes and occludes.'[12] The essential embodiedness of the human person and his or her belonging with others in relation are two crucial factors in the recovery of a notion of spirituality which does not fall prey to the trap of an inner, immaterial Cartesian soul.

Hegel, Marx, Whitehead and Heidegger, whatever their achievements, all failed to dent the influence in the West of radical empiricism and its narrow conception of the self. In wishing to emphasize that human nature is both and equally social and individual, and that unequal emphasis on either leads to a destructive imbalance, there is no better place to start than with the philosophical theology of Paul Tillich and John Macquarrie. Towards the end of his life Reinhold Niebuhr had written eloquently in *Man's Nature and His Communities* about the 'dialectical relation of the individual to the community,[13] but it is in the ontological writings of Tillich and Macquarrie that this 'di-polar' account of human nature is given systematic form. Tillich evolved a doctrine of 'ontological elements' which he claimed were qualities possessed by everything. The first pair of elements was 'individualisation and participation'.[14] On the human level this pair of elements is found as 'person and communion'.[15] Under the conditions of sinful human existence individualization has the tendency to degenerate into 'loneliness', while participation can become 'submergence in the collective'.[16] The gift of salvation which Tillich calls 'New Being' re-establishes the balance between the two poles.[17]

John Macquarrie employs a different set of polar elements (he calls them 'polarities') in his description of human existence, but he agrees with Tillich in affirming a basic polarity within human existence between the individual and society. On the one hand 'sociality' is not 'just something that gets added on when a number of individuals come together'. It is 'intrinsic to human existence', for biologically, economically and linguistically 'the social character of man' is apparent. On the other hand

> Every existence is unique; it is someone's own, unrepeatable and irre-
> placeable. Each human being looks out on the world from the point of
> view of a particular ego and constitutes, as it were, a microcosm. There
> is a privacy about each existence which cannot be quite penetrated even
> by the most sympathetic friend or companion . . . [18]

Like Tillich, Macquarrie speaks of an 'imbalance' between the
polarities, leading to 'disorders' of a social or individual character,
e.g. tyranny or pride,[19] and looks towards the conquest of disorder
in the 'coming together of God and man'.[20]

There are grounds for thinking that radical individualism in moral, religious and economic life has never been as strong as it is
today. If this is so, then emphasis upon the social pole in any
understanding of human nature has never been as important. Any
discussion of the human person is incomplete if it overlooks either
side of the 'community-individuality' polarity and dangerous if it
emphasizes one at the expense of the other. But our principal
concern is with the connections, if any, between the sociality of
human persons and the sociality of the divine Persons of the Holy
Trinity, so let us turn now to the other side of the analogy, and take
as our authoritative statement of the trinitarian doctrine part of the
so-called Athanasian Creed, or *Quicunque vult*, which was written
about the year 500:

> Now the Catholic faith is this: that we should venerate one God in
> Trinity and Trinity in unity,
>   Neither confounding persons nor separating substance.
>   For there is one person of the Father, another of the Son, another of
> the Holy Spirit;
>   But of Father, Son and Holy Spirit one is the divinity, equal the glory,
> co-eternal the majesty . . .
>   In this Trinity there is nothing before or after, nothing greater or less;
> but all three persons are co-eternal with each other and co-equal;
>   So that, in every way unity is to be venerated in Trinity, and Trinity in
> unity.[21]

Is God a person?

The Athanasian Creed does not say that God is a person, and I
have argued elsewhere that it is misleading and dangerous to assume so.[22] Let us again make use of the six types of concept of the
person outlined in chapter 1 in order to see why. The creed affirms
that God is three Persons (and not one), where 'Person' has a
metaphysical sense. We have already noted the misgivings of
Augustine and Aquinas about the application of the term to God,
and so it seems preferable to translate it (with Barth) as three
'modes of being'.[23] Clearly the metaphysical concepts of *hypostasis*
and *persona* are already drawn from the context of application to
human beings, and their use in relation to God must be tentative

and symbolic 'because the supereminence of the Godhead surpasses the power of customary speech'.[24] There are more severe
difficulties with the other types of person concept, and this is because they do not have customary application to God. It is difficult
to speak of God as a unity of mind and body (though possible
perhaps to speak of God and the world in this way). It seems to be
forcing language too far to think of God as acquiring character or
personality except in so far as the human Jesus underwent a real
moral and spiritual growth. God is of course 'an end', and may be
said to treat us as 'ends in ourselves', but talk of means and ends
has its place in moral rather than theological discourse. The existential concept of a person as a self-creating being is intended to
replace God (at least for Sartre) in an atheistic humanism. The
overwhelming weight of use of concepts i) – v) tells against their
application to God. The issue to be explored is whether the social
concept of a person can have useful analogical application to God.

The argument that God is not a person still strikes many people
as odd, plain wrong, or even blasphemous, so it is necessary to
qualify it further. Indeed the assumption that God is a person has
probably contributed much to the decline of influence of the doctrine of the Trinity in Protestant Christianity. The strongest argument for the personhood of God lies with divine action. God is
ceaselessly active. He is said to love us, to have made the world, to
will that certain things should happen, to have sent his Son for our
salvation and to have raised him from the dead, and to be about to
judge all men and women at the end of the age. Essential to the
religious apprehension of God is the presupposition of agency.
God is the great initiative-taker. I claim that what is ontologically
necessary to validate this precondition of theism is the belief that
God is *personal*, not that God is a person.[25] The former alternative
enables us to characterize God as a real, single, divine source of all
being who makes himself known as self-giving Love. And it is a
sufficient precondition for us to experience the divine grace which
reconstitutes and remakes us. We have to speak of him in language
drawn from our own personhood, and it is particularly appropriate
that we should do so, since it is the most important and intimate
language we know. But by affirming that God is personal while
denying that he is a person I hope to have successfully avoided the
unintelligible idea of 'a person without a body' which bedevils
philosophical talk about God, as well as the religious idolatry which
makes God too uncomfortably like human, created persons. Once
it is conceded that it does not harm the religious apprehension of
God to speak in this way, it then becomes possible to build the
personalness of God on a different and theological foundation –
the revelation of God in the person Jesus.

The assumption that God is a personal agent is therefore analogical, and to the extent that it is analogical it is unobjectionable. Even here, though, it is important to point out that the divine analogate of analogies based on human agency is the one Godhead, and so none of the three Persons by themselves: 'But of Father, Son and Holy Spirit, one is the divinity, equal the glory , co-eternal the majesty.' God in his singularity as one indivisible substance (*una substantia*) is not a person, though he is a personal God to whom personal language is properly and analogically applicable. When the language of Scripture, liturgy and devotion declares God's acts or addresses God in the vocative case the 'intentional object' of the language is the Godhead who is at once Father, Son and Spirit. But God's unity is also a tri-unity or trinity, and what the trinity is a trinity of is Persons. But to what extent are the Persons of the Trinity separate beings?

Divine Persons-in-relation

One recent writer is prepared to ascribe to each of the three Persons separate minds and wills. He thinks the unity of God is preserved by the notion of 'generic identity', i.e. Father, Son and Spirit belong to the same *genus*. This *genus* is that of being worthy of worship. There are three beings in this *genus*, but

> they are so intimately related to one another that not only does it make sense to talk of a single reality, the Godhead, but also it is the ultimate reality, in that their unity is such that, though they have separate powers, to know the mind and will of one is to know that of all three.[26]

If this account of the Trinity successfully avoids the charge of tritheism, then clearly we may regard the Persons of the Trinity together as a community or society, but unfortunately it is not clear that the account does avoid this charge. Augustine provides an alternative starting-point with his well-known psychological analogies. His *De Trinitate* employs the method of introspection in order to construct

> a triad of mental acts – the acts of the mind remembering, understanding and willing itself, with special emphasis on the relations of these acts to each other in order to cast light on the eternal divine processions of the Son/Word and of the Holy Spirit from the Father, which constitute the inner mystery of God.[27]

Now we have a different problem. The analogy protects the unity of the Godhead since the one self is the single subject of the mental acts, but these acts themselves may well appear too flimsy to support the doctrine of three distinct Persons in the Godhead. If one approach is in danger of 'separating the substance' the other is in danger of 'confounding the Persons.'

Neither are these two starting-points the only ones available.

Jean Galot, whose use of the concept of the person was analysed in chapter 7, does for the concept of the divine Person what John Macmurray does for the concept of the human person: the divine Persons are 'Persons-in-relation' too. Galot does not use this term, but he says that a person is a 'relational being', and 'When we affirm that the person is a relational being, we are referring to relationship with other persons, to the dynamism of the person orientated toward others.'[28] But what may now come as a surprise is that it is the divine Persons that Galot is thinking of, and not human persons at all. The concept of the Person as a 'relational being' is derived from the relations of the Persons to each other in the Trinity (i.e. the Father is Father to the Son, the Son is Son to the Father, and the Spirit proceeds from both). And if this starting-point is sound then we have a clear and highly effective analogy, not from human persons to the divine Trinity, but in the reverse direction. And Galot seems very confident about its application:

> The divine community of persons in the Trinity is the model of all communities. The Trinity forms the most perfect communion of persons. It is the primordial reason why human beings were created in community . . . Human persons are essentially communitarian. Man and woman were created to be complementary to one another, intrinsically relational to one another, and their community reflects the divine community.[29]

There are obvious difficulties with each of these approaches, though as we shall see shortly the analogical method which has been applied to the Person of Christ so far in this book can also be applied here without the need to take sides or adjudicate between them. If there are three distinct beings in God, all worthy of worship while held together by a generic identity, we do seem to have an 'openly tritheistic God'.[30] Indeed the introduction of the term *genus* in relation to the divine Persons may well invite a comparison with created things which damages the divine unity beyond repair. So much for the social analogy. Is the psychological analogy any better? Hardly. The very attempt of Augustine to construct a trinitarian analogy out of psychological materials lends support to my frequent claim that 'person language' is utterly fundamental to the construction of doctrine, especially the doctrines of God and Christ. But the objection has often been raised against Augustine's use of the psychological analogy that while it protects the unity of God it is not strong enough even to articulate the distinctiveness of the separate Persons. Not only are psychological states not as distinctive from each other as Augustine claims, a mental state of a human person can hardly stand for the constitution of a divine Person. David Brown thinks Augustine's psychological approach cannot commend itself to modern readers because the whole tenor of modern philosophy, especially since Ryle's *Concept of Mind*, has been clearly to move away from a faculty analysis of the human mind towards a dispositional one . . . [where] all talk of faculties becomes essentially arbitrary; there are no entities corresponding to the so-called faculties; they are merely a convenient form of speech which might equally well be replaced by an alternative way of dividing up the mind.[31]

I have taken for granted that this dispositional tenor of modern philosophy provides an important apologetic opportunity for Christian theology, especially Christology, and so I agree with Brown that the different faculties or types of human consciousness are unlikely any longer to be able to stand as working analogies for the divine Persons.

The difficulty with the relational approach to the Trinity is its *a priori* character. From the insight of Augustine and others that Father, Son and Spirit are relational or constituted by their relation to each other (rather than by what each is in itself) it is but a short hop to the claim that human social relations are finite reflections of divine trinitarian relations. We have already noted that in so far as Galot provides an analogy it works in the direction from God to humankind. Therefore, what is perfect or complete or to be emulated about personal relationships can be found to be expressed already in the perfectly relational life of the divine Persons within the Godhead. But this looks to be a speculative doctrine. We can form no clear idea of what it would be like for a trinity of relational beings to coinhere in a divine unity, not least because there is no concrete embodiment of such a pattern in human life as there is of the life of God in the human life of Christ. Unfortunately the concept of 'relational being' or 'subsistent relation' has 'no instantiation in the created order'.[32] But in the created order there are of course human persons-in-relation, and their relationality is central to their identity and their experience, so it does not need to be derived deductively from how the divine Persons are in the Trinity.

Individuality and community – in persons and in God

Despite these difficulties I do not propose to jettison either of these approaches to the Trinity or to adjudicate between the relative merits of each. This is because the argument of earlier chapters has attempted to establish that in the purely human case, the human person is a reality transcending objectifying and causal descriptions. It follows that the meaning of language which is put to work describing inner processes or explaining human actions can never be straightforwardly worked out as adhering to the correspondence theory of truth or the reference theory of meaning. What is more, the great theologians of the Church have in the main displayed a godly reluctance to speak directly of God's incommunicable nature and of the relations between the Persons, and when they have done so they have been well aware of the ontological gap between their language and the divine reality. None the less the doctrine of the Trinity is utterly central to the catholic faith, and like that of the incarnation it cannot be doubted away. My sole reason for discussing the Trinity in this chapter is to inquire whether the analogical approach to the Person of Christ adopted in this book is able to help us to understand something of the mystery of God the Holy Trinity. And at last it is now possible to answer this question directly.

Any personal analogy leading to the divine Trinity differs from our earlier analogies leading to the divine Person of Christ in this important respect: the mystery of the Trinity is a mystery of three Persons and one nature; the mystery of the incarnation is a mystery of one Person and two natures. So I shall not attempt to employ Augustine's psychological analogies in the trinitarian context, having already used more contemporary psychological analogies in the christological context. More importantly, doubt must remain whether a plurality of psychological states can stand for the plurality of Persons within the one God. But if the workings of a single human mind cannot help here, the model of a person-in-relation seems far more promising. It is no longer an internal model which begins with psychological states; it is an external model which takes for granted the fundamental belongingness of individuals to, from, and for each other. The obvious drawback of the model is that individual persons-in-relation are independent centres of consciousness whereas 'In so far as each of the divine persons is distinct from the others he is aware of himself as being thus distinct. Yet he is not aware of being a self in the human sense of the term.'[33]

One contribution which the model of a person-in-relation can make to trinitarian thought is to indicate that the complexities inherent within it have their analogates within anthropology too, and that in each case, the anthropological and the trinitarian, living with the difficulties is far more satisfactory than the impatient reduction of the complex to the simple. An adequate understanding of human persons has to encompass both the individual and the social poles of human existence. Earlier in this chapter it was observed that some theologians think the disruption of the poles is a consequence of sin. But it is equally important to emphasize that the two poles, even in their disrupted state, still require each other, for human existence is alike dependent, independent, and interdependent. An approach to the person which concentrates exclusively upon individuality simply neglects the communal dimension, and this neglect is easily institutionalized in the dominant values and language of a culture. Excessive concentration on the communal dimension can all too readily overlook basic rights and freedoms, and indeed we may speculate that outside of the Kingdom of God a perfect balance between the individual and the social poles of human existence does not exist. But, and this is the heart of the matter, in God it *does* exist. And the doctrine of the Trinity is the classical and indispensable way of expressing it.

Finally let us explore how our analogy might be developed both from humankind to God and back. The starting-point for the analogy 'from below' is the model of a person-in-relation. This model will embrace both poles of human existence. The individual who comes to be was first created and sustained by others and depends on others now, on their work and their companionship, for the maintenance and quality of life. The language each person comes to acquire is not his or her own, nor is the culture he inherits. Relationality is never more obvious than in regard for the other, for the other's sake, i.e. in and through love. The mutuality and reciprocity of being in love, and the response of love towards those whose circumstances prohibit any mutual or reciprocal response, provide obvious examples of human relationality. That is why Christian commentators may justly point out (whatever the original meaning of the unknown author) that the image of God in Genesis 1.26–8 is shared equally by men and women, i.e. they are not made in the image of God in their individuality; rather humankind is made in God's image, and that is why humankind is male and female.

There now lies exposed another reason why great caution must be exercised in holding God to be a person, as so much popular literature does. Reflection on the procedure always shows up how the 'bodiless person' which God is presumed to be has its origin in the Western model of the human individual person.[34] But persons are not merely individuals unrelated to other persons; their relationality as well as their materiality is jettisoned when they are made to do duty for a disembodied Mind, Spirit, Agent or Self. Persons are persons-in-relation, and a person-in-relation is a much better model for what Christians mean by God than the individual conveniently abstracted from others for the scholarly purpose of model-making. Persons-in-relation, as Elizabeth Moberly has movingly written, live *from* each other and *for* each other in mutual interdependence.[35] Within the interdependence great potentialities exist for both good and evil. Without interdependence human love in all its forms, and the mutual enrichment which daily life makes possible, would be impossible. In God, the divine Persons are also in relation. It may be assumed that their relations with each other constitute an unimaginable plenitude of holy love from which all work of creation, redemption and sanctification proceeds. There is individuality and society in God in a manner perfectly appropriate to that unfathomable personal reality which he is and which human persons-in-relation 'image' in their social and relational being.

How might the analogy work 'from above', from the Trinity to humankind? Can we say with Jean Galot that 'the divine community of persons in the Trinity is the model of all communities'?[36] Or with Elizabeth Moberly that the life of God within the Trinity is a basic pattern of life *for* others and *from* others, so providing created human life with its norm and exemplification? I think there are two qualifications to be made. First, statements about the trinitarian life of God, despite their appearance in scholastic textbooks, do not have to be *a priori*. They derive from the revelation of God in and through the Son, from the experience of God through the Spirit, and from the long tradition of the worship of, and reflection upon, God as Father, Son and Spirit. The doctrine of the Trinity is the culmination of all monotheism, given only after centuries of godly learning. In this sense, then, it is not *a priori*, since it is itself the product of the Christian revelation and the experience of the Church whose doctrine it is. Second, the character of our language about Persons and relations is transcended by the mysteries it attempts to describe. Of course there is hardly a version of Christian theism anywhere which does not make such a qualification. But the journey through this book has given reasons for grounding the appropriate tentativeness of talk about the divine Persons in the appropriate tentativeness of talk about human persons, where there is also much mystery and relationality. Language about ourselves and our states has a real, though indirect, reference, and the argument of chapter 5 suggested that much religious language can be modelled on 'person language'. Trinitarian analogies are doubtless more complex and therefore more fraught with difficulties than christological ones, and thus will be more tentative in their construction and application. The twentieth-century understanding of persons-in-relation is likely to be an indispensable aid in the task.

NOTES

1 Alasdair MacIntyre, *After Virtue* (London: Duckworth, 1981), p. 212.
2 Jeremy Bentham, *An Introduction to the Principles of Morals and Legislation* (1780), cit. Stuart Brown, *Introduction to Philosophy*, Open University Arts Foundation Course A102, Unit 13 (Milton Keynes: Open University Press, 1986), p. 13. Author's emphasis.
3 MacIntyre, *After Virtue*. The sustained criticism makes selection difficult. The first eight chapters are essential reading.
4 John Macmurray, *Persons in Relation* (London: Faber & Faber, 1961), ch. 1.
5 See Peter Singer, *Marx* (Oxford University Press, 1980), ch. 2.
6 See Peter Singer, *Hegel* (Oxford University Press, 1983), p. 34.

7   A. N. Whitehead, *Adventures of Ideas* (Cambridge: Cambridge University Press, 1933), pp. 263–4.

8   Karl Marx, *Economic-Philosophical Manuscripts* (1844), cit. A. Clayre (ed.), *Nature and Industrialization* (Oxford: Oxford University Press, 1977), p. 248.

9   M. Heidegger, *Being and Time*, tr. J. Macquarrie and E. Robinson (Oxford: Basil Blackwell, 1962), p. 44.

10 ibid., 1.1.2.

11 Ably led by Fergus Kerr. See his *Theology After Wittgenstein* (Oxford: Basil Blackwell, 1986).

12 ibid., pp. 89–90 (emphasis added).

13 Niebuhr, *Man's Nature and His Communities* (London: Geoffrey Bles, 1966), p. 81.

14 Paul Tillich, *Systematic Theology, Volume 1* (Digswell Place: Nisbet, 1953), pp. 193.

15 ibid., p. 195.

16 Paul Tillich, *Systematic Theology, Volume 2* (Digswell Place: Nisbet, 1957), pp. 75–6.

17 Or so Tillich claims. See my *The Ontology of Paul Tillich* (Oxford: Oxford University Press, 1978), p. 151.

18 John Macquarrie, *Principles of Christian Theology* (London: SCM Press, ²1977), p. 67. In the earlier version of this volume the polarity is that between *community* and individuality. In the later version 'community' is more associated with social relationships which are not disordered by sin.

19 ibid., p. 69.

20 ibid., p. 301.

21 Text in, e.g., Edmund Hill OP, *The Mystery of the Trinity* (London: Geoffrey Chapman, 1985), p. 5.

22 Adrian Thatcher, 'The Personal God and a God who is a Person', *Religious Studies*, xxi (1985), pp. 61–73; Adrian Thatcher, 'Christian Theism and the Concept of a Person' in Arthur Peacocke and Grant Gillett (eds), *Persons and Personality* (Oxford: Basil Blackwell, 1987), ch. 12.

23 Karl Barth, *Church Dogmatics*, tr. G. W. Bromiley (Edinburgh: T. & T. Clark, ²1975), 1.1.2.

24 Augustine, *De Trinitate*, 7.4.7. Above, ch. 1. p. 7.

25 Thatcher, 'The Personal God and God who is a Person', p. 71.

26 David Brown, *The Divine Trinity* (London: Duckworth, 1985), p. 293.

27 Edmund Hill, *The Mystery of the Trinity*, p. 80, et seq. The analogy is found in *De Trinitate* 10. Book 9 contains another psychological analogy, that of mind, knowledge and love.

28 Jean Galot SJ, *Who is Christ? A Theology of the Incarnation* (Rome: Gregorian University Press, 1980), p. 298.

29 ibid., p. 301.

30 See Alan Lewis's review of *The Divine Trinity*, *Scottish Journal of Theology*, xl (1987), p. 559.

31 Brown, *The Divine Trinity*, p. 273.

32 H. P. Owen, *Christian Theism* (Edinburgh: T. & T. Clark, 1984), p. 62.

33 ibid., p. 63.

34 I dub this 'bodiless person theism', which operates by means of a 'dematerializing procedure'. See Thatcher, 'The Personal God and God who is a Person', §§2 & 3. Support for this approach comes from D. W. D. Shaw, 'Personality, Personal and Person' in A. Kee and E. T. Long (eds), *Being and Truth: Essays in Honour of John Macquarrie* (London: SCM Press, 1986).

35 Elizabeth Moberly, *Suffering, Innocent and Guilty* (London: Darton, Longman & Todd, 1978), chapter 7.

36 Galot, *Who is Christ?*, p. 301.

CHAPTER 11

Personal Knowledge and Divine Love

Previous chapters have developed various analogies which have begun with the human person and moved towards the Person of Christ or, as in the last chapter, the triune God. This final chapter begins not with a model of the person, but with personal *knowledge*, and asks whether personal knowledge is able to indicate something of the nature of our knowledge of God. The discussion of personal knowledge, together with elements from the discussion of identity in chapter 4, will then enable further insights into the basic Christian claim about God, that 'God is love' (1 John 4.8,16), to be attempted.

Personal knowledge and faith

Let us now turn to the human knowledge of God and inquire whether the concept of a person can provide pointers here. Of the six person-concepts which have been listed, the sixth, or person-in-relation, will again be the most useful. I take it for granted that God is a 'real object' to be known, and therefore that knowledge of him is more than a set of psychological states, and that he is more than some 'formal', 'notional' or 'intentional' object towards which consciousness is directed. God is a community of infinite divine Persons. God is the supreme creative personal reality, individual in the fullness of his being, communal in his Personhood, a God who acts, who may be spoken of by personal analogies, and who has from the depths of his love for the world become incarnate in the human person Jesus. As chapter 6 put the matter, in Jesus the divine subject appears in person; the hidden God is now unhidden, unelusive and explicitly identifiable.

The knowledge of God is a form of personal knowledge. It is surely defensible, following the work of Martin Buber, John Macmurray, Michael Polanyi, John Macquarrie and others, to posit 'personal knowledge' as a basic category of knowledge,[1] not least because some of the knowledge we acquire of other people cannot be classified into either knowledge of things or knowledge of truths.[2] Let us make use of the familiar contrast between propositional and personal knowledge, and observe that the content of the former is factual and is expressed by true propositions, while the content of the latter is other persons and is expressed in the form of relationships with them. Since some of the details of personal knowledge are statable in propositional form, the two types are not exclusive.

John Hick recalls that there are two traditional words for 'faith', *fides* and *fiducia*. *Fides* means

> faith that there is a God and that such and such propositions about him are true. Here 'faith' is used cognitively . . . On the other hand, we speak of faith (*fiducia*) as a trust, maintained sometimes despite contrary indications, that the divine purpose toward us is wholly good and loving. This is a religious trust which may be *compared with trust or confidence in another human person*.[3]

Much knowledge of other persons is at the level of acquaintance and is objective, especially when we meet them in public contexts like queues, traffic jams and tube trains. At other times our relationships are purely functional, as in economic or bureaucratic transactions. In so far as it is proper to speak of knowledge of other persons at all under these conditions, the knowledge acquired is superficial and propositional, describable, we may say, by means of M-predicates. The potentially personal character of relationships is very largely suspended under these conditions, and each person becomes for the other more like a material object than a person, or loses himself in a social role, like Sartre's café waiter.[4] At other times social roles may become discarded altogether and one person may respond to another not simply as a consumer, client, co-user of public transport and the like, but as a person whose company, friendship, and perhaps even love, is wanted mutually, for its own sake, and for no reason extrinsic to the relationship. Ian Ramsey used to call such situations 'discernment situations', i.e. 'characteristically personal' situations where 'the ice breaks', 'the penny drops', and so on. These, he said, were analogous to religious discernment.[5] As persons we enjoy our lives with others and express the enjoyment in our relationships, expectations of them, obligations to them, and so on. This personal knowledge of others, acquired in relationships and stated by means of P-predicates or avowals, can be fairly contrasted with propositional knowledge of the objective world.

Let us now examine that element of trust which can sometimes become a valued component of personal knowledge. Hick is wrong to imply that only propositional knowledge is cognititve, for there is much cognitive content in personal knowledge too. When it begins to occur it already assumes a developed interpersonal context, which will have involved a good deal of openness and mutuality. Now the knowledge of God-in-person is personal knowledge in that it also involves trust. The knowledge this time is not knowledge of another but is instead of God-in-person. It is of 'the Son of

God, who loved me and gave himself up for me' (Galatians 2.20).
Elements of this knowledge can usefully be brought into focus by
using three pairs of contrasts. The knowledge of God-in-person is
interpretative rather than inferential; *holistic* rather than mentalistic;
and *contemplative* rather than controlling. All three are grounded in
personal knowledge.

The function of P-predicates is to *interpret* the states of persons.[6]
With personal knowledge a richer notion of interpretation can be
found. Suppose 'I' have a close friend, and our relationship is
sustained by the exchange of letters and presents, regular meetings,
phone calls, and so on. Knowing this person to be a friend does not
consist in drawing inferences from his or her behaviour towards me
that he is my friend or I am his friend. If it did, then his behaviour
towards me would be evidence for something else and the experience of friendship would be like holding a hypothesis. Doubting
the friendship would be like doubting, when confronted with a real
case, whether a person in pain was in pain.[7] The knowledge that he
is a friend rests in the experience of the meetings, exchanges of
confidences, and so on, and is therefore non-inferential. However,
it is interpretative, in that the knowledge which is stated by 'He is
my friend' already combines much direct experience with due reflection upon it, so that the use of the concept 'friend' in connection with this particular person is already an interpretation. It is a
way of talking about enjoying his company, sharing interests, etc.,
and not something in addition to these things.

The importance of interpretation as an element of the human
knowledge of God is a familiar theme in philosophical theology.
John Hick's well-known essay 'Religious Faith as Experiencing-as'
proposed 'a conception of faith as the *interpretative* element within
our cognitive religious experience', based on Wittgenstein's treatment of alternative responses to puzzle pictures and ambiguous
diagrams like the Necker cube, Jastrow's duck-rabbit, and Kohler's
goblet-faces.[8] John Smith has used the idea of 'interpreted experience' to provide what he calls a 'third alternative' to accounts of
religious experience which avoid the attempts on the one hand to
identify our consciousness of God with the 'immediate data of
experience' and on the other to draw inferences leading to God
from a world in which the divine reality is not experienced at all.[9] A
similar position, that of 'mediated immediacy', is found in John
Baillie's classic study *Our Knowledge of God*.[10] These studies are
valuable, but they can now be supplemented with a more adequate
notion of personal interpretation.

Knowledge of other people and knowledge of God

Before the comparison between our knowledge of other people and
our knowledge of God is developed, there is a danger to be avoid-

ed. A misleading epistemological framework can suggest itself, within which human knowledge of God can be described as an attempt to know a superperson who lacks a body. Once the problem has been set in this way the analogies drawn from personal knowledge which attempt to illuminate our knowledge of God inevitably get misinterpreted as providing comparisons between other living persons with whom we are in relationship and an invisible divine person whose lack of embodiment vitiates the analogy even before its completion. The firmest ground for belief in a personal God is that, through the incarnation, when Jesus speaks and acts, God speaks and acts through him. Human personal knowledge requires non-inferential interpretation of the facts of lived relationships, as when the attitudes of friends and loved ones, we might say, 'speak for themselves'. An analogy worth developing now comes into view, between our knowledge of other persons in relation with us and our knowledge of the God who chooses to reveal himself in the person Jesus. This analogy is stronger than it first appears. For what is interpreted is the entire life and teaching of Jesus, and his crucifixion and resurrection as God's infallible declaration of love towards his creation. Instead of the behaviour of another human person towards 'me', which I interpret as constituting friendship, there is the behaviour of Jesus Christ towards the common people of Palestine, which the Church interprets as the mind or attitude or heart of God towards all men and women everywhere. What was objectively there in space and time to be interpreted was a historical life. For the disciples Jesus was literally a person-in-relation.

The centrality of God's revelation in the Christ-event does not diminish the freedom of God to become revealed in other ways. The human act of interpreting God's revelation is poorly represented by the perceptual task of making sense of puzzle pictures or of coming to a philosophical decision about which of the several cosmologies currently on offer is marginally the more probable. That is why the human knowledge of God is primarily *holistic*, i.e. it is acquired by persons as wholes. The term is somewhat fashionable at present, especially in ecology, psychology and medicine, but it can be usefully drawn into epistemology as well. It was used in the title of chapter 9. Holistic knowledge occurs when intellectual capacities combine with affective and conative ones so that what is known requires the participation of the subject as a whole in what he or she knows, and the apprehension of the known involves to greater or lesser degrees the combination of, say, feeling, understanding, willing and imagining. By contrast, mentalistic knowledge is acquired primarily by intellection alone, and need not significantly involve the wider range of human responses as in holistic knowledge. It is especially appropriate to a Cartesian *res cogitans*. It may take the form of a passive assimilation of facts or a more active engagement of the intellect in, say, problem-solving or performing experiments.

Knowledge of other persons again provides the principal context for locating the holistic element of our knowledge of God, while moral and aesthetic knowledge also come close. The intellect has only a limited part to play in acquiring knowledge of another person, for persons do not present themselves as intellectual problems to be solved, facts to be assimilated, data to be processed or ideas to be grasped. They are co-persons to be known in mutuality. In opening oneself to another, one acts as the total person one is, using intellect, imagination, volition and empathy appropriately so that the activity which one engages in when coming to know another person is not primarily an activity of mind but an activity of the person as a totality. The giving and receiving of love is the most valuable form of holistic knowledge, and love is the mode *par excellence* of human knowledge of God. Its holistic character is illustrated by the first commandment of Jesus, to 'love the Lord your God with all your heart, with all your soul, with all your mind, and with all your strength' (Mark 12.30). The response to God clearly has to be understood along the lines of the response to a person whom one loves (for how else is 'loving God' to be understood?), even though it must transcend it. And that response is obviously holistic, involving (as the text plainly insists) the full range of intentional, emotional, cognitive and conative states of the person. Again the contrast between personal and propositional knowledge is mirrored, for whereas the knowledge of God derivable from theology is more mentalistic, involving reflection and intellection, the worship of God is clearly a holistic act for both the worshipper and the congregation. Not only does the worship of God involve all five of the senses, it requires the appropriate exercise of intellect, feeling, imagination and will, and it integrates them in the apprehension of the object of worship. Through worship, Christians say, God also addresses us, and we may speculate that through the engagement of all our senses and capacities we are addressed as whole persons. More appropriately in this context we should say we are addressed as children of God.

The human knowledge of God is also *contemplative* rather than 'controlling'. With 'controlling knowledge' (a term borrowed from Paul Tillich) the knower dominates what is known and manipulates and utilizes it for his or her own purposes. Controlling knowledge

is the outstanding, though not the only, example of technical reason. It unites subject and object for the sake of the control of the object by the subject. It transforms the object into a completely conditioned and calculable 'thing'. It deprives it of any subjective quality. Controlling knowledge looks upon its object as something which cannot return its look.[11]

With contemplative knowledge the knower contemplates but does not control: he stands at the boundary between knowledge and what is beyond knowledge. In contemplation one knows that one does not know. One gains a sensitivity to mystery and a positive appreciation of it. This appreciation of the limits to knowledge reflects back upon the intellect, reminding it of its fallibility and the relative puniness of its achievements.

Much has been written recently about sensitivity to mystery and its role in religious thought.[12] It has been fruitfully linked with the phenomena of wonder and awe, particularly with the wonder that there is a world at all; but the linkage to be established here is with personal knowledge. The discussion of anomalous monism in chapter 8 led to the suggestion that 'on the human level there are whole areas of our life which stubbornly refuse causal explanation, third-person observation and scientific objectification', and that 'there is a baffling mystery, coupled with an extreme immediacy about how both conscious states and their relation to physical states are understood'.[13] It is but a small shift to transfer these transcending qualities of a person from the first-person perspective to the other whom one knows in relation. That is, the closer 'I' become to another the more seriously I must take his or her being as a person, and the more seriously I do this, the greater is the obligation neither to attempt to possess the other, nor to dominate, nor to exercise power over the responses of the other to myself. Control is replaced by reciprocation. (Even in the care of children the use of control can normally be lessened progressively.) In close personal relationships a fundamental element is the recognition of the final impenetrability of the other, and thus of the hidden depths of the other's being which for 'me' must ever be screened off and remain a mystery. That is why the word 'contemplative' can be used in the context of personal knowledge. Before the other with whom I am close, I am trustingly receptive; I am 'still' in the face of our mutual openness; and I 'marvel' at the unity between us.

Contemplative knowledge is clearly a major element of the Christian knowledge of God-in-person. Not only can God not be controlled or dominated, God does not control or dominate his people (as the familiar monarchical images of God once suggested), but instead God in Christ acts to bestow on men and women 'life . . . in all its fullness' (John 10.10). The incarnation is itself a 'coming close', to the point of identification, a divine movement forwards and outwards to human others in unbounded love. At no point does God coerce the other into a response, for God-in-person acts towards us more like a ' cosmic lover'[14] than a cosmic ruler. Rather the response of faith is elicited, not controlled, and this is analogous to the trusting response which arises in the close human relation. The wonder which the other evokes in personal knowledge has its theological counterpart in the experience of grace. What happens to the recipient is uncontrolled, unanticipated and undeserved. In an analogous way, believers interpret Jesus Christ as God's initiative, intervening on their behalf, without right and without merit remaking them and fulfilling their created potentialities, nudging them towards that which God intends them to be.

Ordinarily, accounts of personal knowledge assume, however, that the persons who are known are living, embodied and materially present in the world. The historical Jesus of Nazareth cannot satisfy these conditions for us, though they were satisfied for his disciples who believed in him. But once the idea of 'interpreted experience', itself an element of personal knowledge, is accepted, Christian faith can readily accommodate this difficulty, for it asserts that the person Jesus is alive, and it locates him firmly in the Church and in the world. Jesus, it was suggested in chapter 9, is he whose wholeness and sinlessness make available new patterns of personalness. These patterns, because they are non-natural (i.e. we cannot produce them ourselves), are rightly said to be given by God the Spirit. Christ is said to be alive wherever the disruptive elements of human existence are overcome and reconciled by the power which remakes all things by making them whole. His body or corporate presence in the world, Christians say, has two forms. It is the people who live his compassion (the Church), or it is those who, like the poor and oppressed, await compassionate action (Matthew 25.31–46). The knowledge of God, then, is not to be found in some special intuition of a divine super-person, but is rather knowledge of that divine power which manifests itself transformingly in individual and social humanness, making for increasing wholeness and fulfilled personal life. God-in-person is a real epistemological 'object', and attempts to articulate 'it' more concisely are likely to require a transition from the language of philosophy to that of religious faith, where it is depicted through expressions such as 'the power of the Spirit', 'the risen Christ', 'life in the Spirit', 'Christian fellowship', and so on. Like all personal knowledge, the knowledge of God is acquired by sharing. The experiential dimension of our knowledge is not of course the whole of it, but it has been much neglected, especially among writers who hold that the fundamental essence of the person is mind.

The ontology of love – human and divine

Can the themes of this book contribute anything to our comprehension of the divine love? I shall make five brief suggestions. First, the distinction made in chapter 4 between identity of reference and difference of meaning, which was useful for analysing 'Jesus is God the Son', is useful here when reflecting upon the meaning of the biblical statement 'God is love' (1 John 4.8, 16). Let us take 'God is love' as an identity statement, treat it like the earlier statement 'Jesus is God the Son', and examine the terms 'God' and 'love' for identity of reference and difference of meaning. Given that Christians discern Jesus Christ as God-in-person, both 'God' and 'love' refer to what is shown through Jesus Christ. They have a common reference. Provided that Jesus Christ is the criterion for assessing what is to count as love, then God is love and love is God. Love, bodied forth in the life and death of Jesus, is the same as God. Of course here love is not understood as human affection, friendship or desire.[15] God's love, by contrast,

> is not attracted by some lovable quality, it is poured out on those who are worthless and degraded . . . This Divine Love turns to those for whom no one cares, because there is nothing 'lovable' about them . . . Here the One who loves does not seek anything for Himself; all He desires is to benefit the one he loves.[16]

The reversed statement 'love is God' also looks to be in accord with its biblical context, the first letter of John, which insists that everyone who hates his or her brother or sister is a murderer, that love must show itself in action, that everyone who loves is a child of God and knows God, that the unloving know nothing of God, that he who dwells in love is dwelling in God and God in him, and so on. 'Love', then, is no abstract noun waiting to be given a meaning. Rather is it the term which for Christians derives its meaning from Jesus Christ; and, since Jesus is God's Son, it is also confidently affirmed to be the nature of God. 'Love' interprets the life, death and resurrection of Jesus as no other word can. As we saw in chapter 6, the appearance of God-in-person was contrasted with the personification of God through, say the divine Wisdom or Word. 'Love is God' is similarly no personification of God, as it is in the carol 'Love came down at Christmas'. It identifies God's nature with the self-giving of Jesus. 'God is love' answers the questions 'What is love?' and 'What is God?' After Jesus the two are interdefinable. But the kind of identity which is suggested here does not exclude the many verbal uses of 'God' and 'love' where identity would not be claimed. The reason for this is that the identity which operates here, like that which operates within the concept of the person, allows for difference of meaning as well as identity of reference.

Second, the concept of love which is identical with God's nature must therefore be ontological. Recognition of its character puts a definitional stop on accounts of God's love which reduce it to a human quality writ large, and then apply it to God symbolically. Reductive tendencies can occur here, just as they occurred in materialist accounts of persons. Ontology again stops the reductive slide, this time with the ontological concept of love. This concept, which alone is identifiable with God, cannot reduce to popular sentimental accounts of love. So, for example, where love is primarily an emotional concept the power of the emotion can become an independent object of desire separate from the loved one. Where love is a moralizing concept it can lead to a dubious obligation to engage in philanthropic activity which leads merely to a temporary salving of the conscience. Where love is a social concept it is likely to be based on mutual interests and attractiveness, elements which automatically exclude the unattractive and the unloved. Even where love is a religious concept it can lead to a supposed love-relation with God the Father or Jesus the Son with all the attendant psychological dangers of the deity becoming a virtual surrogate lover or compensator for failed human relationships. By contrast the irreducible love of God brought into the world through the being of Jesus, a love which accepts the unacceptable, exposes human cruelty and prejudice by submitting itself to them, and identifies with victims of all kinds of misery and suffering, is of another order. It provides the criteria for assessing all other loves.

Third, the ontological concept of love is capable of providing an interpretation of the whole of finite being as having a love-making character. Just as the culmination of organic life in human persons is historically and theologically a preparation for the coming of God-in-person, so the crucifixion of Christ is the culmination of human love and the revelation of divine love in one perfect life. This life, for Christians, is the beginning of a new creation, a Spirit-given reality which is the fulfilment of created being. Within the context of the new creation the narrow first-person perspective on love falls away, and love as a shared social reality is dreamed of instead. No longer is love seen merely from the individual stance, where 'I' reach out, become involved, get rebuffed, and so on; instead it is where *agape* becomes a social norm. The perspective upon the world which makes such a reality even conceivable is God's, for as Spirit God acts to bring about a human community where the poles of individuality and sociality are transcended in an integrated humanity. Such a view of humankind is theologically a 'vision', a 'hope' (celebrated in the anticipatory character of the

Eucharist). But hope for the future can be reflected back into the present to mould present aims and choices, and the present unrealizability of the hope should not weaken the striving to bring it about. 'Dreaming' and 'envisioning' have their proper place in holistic thinking, belonging to the realm of imagination. In the love which belongs with faith and hope individuality and communality at last belong together.

Fourth, there are several features of personal knowledge which may illuminate our understanding of God's love, though we must be careful to recognize both comparison and contrast when bringing them together. Norman Pittenger is scarcely the first Christian writer to suggest that sexual passion can provide an analogue for God's love, when he writes that 'the passionate intensity which in our limited and defective way is known in human sexuality must characterise his [God's] nature'.[17] 'Knowledge' in the biblical languages can mean penetration in a sexual as well as a purely perceptual sense.[18] It has already been suggested that in loving relationships the freedom of the other must always be acknowledged, and that an indication of love lies in the refusal of any attempt to control the other person. So in creating persons who possess freedom (as opposed to puppet-like creatures over whom he has full, if veiled, control), God provides also for the freedom of creatures not to respond, or to respond negatively. On the human level, reaching out towards another person involves the risk of rebuff, misunderstanding and hurt, and, so the suggestion runs, making a world is for God a monumental risk which the divine love accepts, for without risk there would be no out-going in love and no possibility of loving response, either for God or for ourselves. The rebuff which God may be said to receive does not alter the divine attitude towards humankind; rather God's preparedness to suffer rejection becomes an intimation of the supreme value he places on a loving union with creatures. Arthur Peacocke has tentatively suggested that 'God's acts of creation – the interplay of risky chance and law-like necessity in the creative processes of the cosmos, in relation to which God stands as agent – are an expression of "love", an outgoing of his inner being on behalf of another, albeit created, person.'[19]

When agency is attributed to God, we recall, the divine subject is the one Godhead and so the action is the action of all three Persons. We may claim then, fifthly, that personal knowledge is a dim analogue of the trinitarian relations within God which were discussed in chapter 10. The trinitarian doctrine bequeathes a vision of God who in his perfect personal being transcends finite distinctions between individuality and sociality: that being is eternally constituted as Love in its internal relationships. From this divine love, that which is other than God is created in order to become the beloved recipients of and participants in such love. The shared love which constitutes and sustains persons-in-relation may, within the limitations mentioned in the last chapter, be seen to be a finite reflection of that infinite relational love within God which bursts forth into the making and redeeming of the world.

The personal knowledge which issues in love provides us with the experiences and concepts which enable us to speak of God's redeeming love for us. On the other hand, while human love can grow cold, divine love endures forever; while human love is selective, divine love excludes no one. The difference is that 'Christ died for us while we were yet sinners, and that is God's own proof of his love towards us' (Romans 5.8). But the qualitative difference between God's infinite love and our finite love does not invalidate the analogy, for the material drawn from the human side is only a means of aiding that contemplation of God's love which surpasses knowledge. Jesus, it will be recalled, used the finest human love to model divine love when he taught his disciples 'There is no greater love than this, that a man should lay down his life for his friends' (John 15.13).

When I began this study I was initially nervous about the weight which was being placed on analogy. Would not the temptation to demonstrate rather than illustrate, to establish rather than suggest, become irresistible? But as the study proceeded I grew more confident in both the method and the content as it began to unfold. There just *are* comparisons to be explored between the reality which is a human person and that reality which is confessed as God's eternal Son, and these comparisons lead naturally from being, through knowledge, to love, and from individuality to community in humankind and in God. The exploration has been a most rewarding one to undertake, and if, at a time when there is renewed interest in the intelligibility of Christian claims about Jesus, it has developed any partial insights into that inexhaustible mystery which is God in Christ, then I have been doubly rewarded.

NOTES

1 For an illuminating discussion of personal knowledge, see John Macquarrie, *In Search of Humanity* (London: S C M Press, 1982), ch. 6.
2 i.e., Bertrand Russell's influential classification in his *The Problems of Philosophy* (Oxford: Oxford University Press, 10th imp. 1982, 1st pub. 1912), pp. 62–3.
3 John Hick, *Faith and Knowledge* (Glasgow: Collins Fontana, ²1974), p. 3, emphasis added.
4 Jean-Paul Sartre, *Being and Nothingness*, tr. Hazel Barnes (London: Methuen, 1969), p. 59.
5 Ian T. Ramsey, *Religious Language* (New York: Macmillan Paperbacks, 1963, 1st pub. 1957), ch. 1.

6 Above, pp. 59–60.
7 L. Wittgenstein, *Philosophical Investigations*, tr. G. E. M. Anscombe (Oxford: Basil Blackwell, 1972, 1st pub. 1953), §303.
8 John Hick, *God and the Universe of Faiths* (Glasgow: Collins Fount, [2]1977), p. 49. And see Wittgenstein, *Philosophical Investigations*, part 2, §11. J. G. Davies works with a similar religious epistemology. See his *Everyday God* (London: SCM Press, 1973), p. 30.
9 John E. Smith, *Experience and God* (New York: Oxford University Press, 1968), p. 52.
10 John Baillie, *Our Knowledge of God* (London: Oxford University Press, 1963, 1st pub. 1939), ch. 16.
11 Paul Tillich, *Systematic Theology, Volume 1* (Digswell Place: Nisbet, 1953), pp. 108–9.
12 For two outstanding contributions see 'Appendix: On the Meanings of "Mystery" ' in H. J. K. Schilling, *The New Consciousness in Science and Religion* (London: SCM Press, 1973), pp 267–76; and John Macquarrie, *Thinking About God* (London: SCM Press, 1975), ch. 3.
13 Above, p. 103.
14 Norman Pittenger's term. See, e.g., his *The Christian Church as Social Process* (London: Epworth Press, 1971), p. 5.
15 As Plato saw (*Symposium*, §199–203), love understood as desire could never be applied to God because desire cannot happen without a lack, and God lacks nothing.
16 Emil Brunner, *The Christian Doctrine of God* (London: Lutterworth Press, 5th imp., 1962), p. 186.
17 Norman Pittenger, *Christology Reconsidered* (London: SCM Press, 1970), p. 129.
18 As Erich Fromm notes in his popular *To Have Or To Be?* (London: Jonathan Cape, Abacus Books, 1978), pp. 48–9.
19 Arthur Peacocke, *Science and the Christian Experiment* (Oxford: Clarendon Press, 1979), p. 199.

Index